About the Authors

LT. GEN. HAROLD G. MOORE (USA RET.), eighty-seven, was born in Kentucky. A West Point graduate, Moore was a master parachutist and army aviator, commanded two infantry companies in the Korean War, and was a battalion and brigade commander in Vietnam. He retired from the Army in 1977 with thirty-two years' service, and served as executive vice president of a Colorado ski resort for four years before founding a computer software company. Moore lives in Auburn, Alabama.

JOSEPH L. GALLOWAY, sixty-seven, is a native of Refugio, Texas. The author of a weekly syndicated column on military and national-security affairs, he recently retired as senior military correspondent of Knight Ridder Newspapers. Galloway was a special consultant to Gen. Colin Powell at the State Department in 2001 and 2002. Galloway spent twenty-two years as a foreign and war correspondent and bureau chief for United Press International, and nearly twenty years as a senior editor and senior writer for *U.S. News & World Report*. He lives in Bayside, Texas.

ALSO BY LT. GEN. HAROLD G. MOORE

AND JOSEPH L. GALLOWAY

We Were Soldiers Once . . . and Young

Lt. Gen. Harold G. Moore (USA ret.)

and Joseph L. Galloway

HARPER PERENNIAL

NEW YORK • LONDON • TORONTO • SYDNEY • NEW DELHI • AUCKLAND

WE ARE
SOLDIERS
STILL

A Journey Back to the
Battlefields of Vietnam

HARPER ● PERENNIAL

A hardcover edition of this book was published in 2008
by HarperCollins Publishers.

HarperCollins books may be purchased for educational,
business, or sales promotional use. For information please write:
Special Markets Department, HarperCollins Publishers,
10 East 53rd Street, New York, NY 10022.

FIRST HARPER PERENNIAL EDITION PUBLISHED 2009.

Designed by Kara Strubel

Frontispiece courtesy of Getty Images.

The Library of Congress has catalogued the hardcover edition
as follows:

Moore, Harold G.
We are soldiers still : a journey back to the battlefields of Vietnam /
   by Harold G. Moore and Joseph L. Galloway. —1st ed.
   p. cm.
   Includes index.
   ISBN 978-0-06-114776-0
   1. Moore, Harold G., 1922– —Travel—Vietnam. 2. Galloway,
Joseph L.—Travel—Vietnam. 3. Vietnam War, 1961–1975—Battle-
fields. 4. Ia Drang Valley, Battle of, Vietnam, 1965. 5. Vietnam—
Description and travel.
DS557.7.M64   2008
959.704'342—dc22   2008011034

ISBN 978-0-06-114777-7 (pbk.)

09 10 11 12 13 ID/RRD 10 9 8 7 6 5 4 3 2 1

This book is dedicated
to the memory of two who loved us best:

Julia Compton Moore
1929–2004

Theresa Null Galloway
1948–1996

CONTENTS

Foreword by Gen. H. Norman Schwarzkopf   XI

Preface   XV

CHAPTER 1   *Back to Our Battlefields*   1

CHAPTER 2   *Conversations with the Enemy*   19

CHAPTER 3   *You Killed My Battalion!*   41

CHAPTER 4   *Traveling in Time*   53

CHAPTER 5   *The Backbone of the Army*   71

CHAPTER 6   *Back to the Ia Drang!*   83

CHAPTER 7   *A Night Alone on the Battlefield*   101

CHAPTER 8   *Back to the Hell That Was Albany*   113

CHAPTER 9   *Walking the Ground at Dien Bien Phu*   129

CHAPTER 10   *The Never-Ending Story*   147

CHAPTER 11   *Lessons on Leadership*   157

CHAPTER 12   *On War*   187

Epilogue   199

Appendix: Two Heroes for America   203

Acknowledgments   227

An Appeal   231

Index   233

Photography Credits   247

FOREWORD

For each generation and each war there is a defining book that tells the story and recaptures the experience of those who fought that war with such accuracy and truth that old veterans read it through tears and cherish it as a prized possession. My old, good friends Hal Moore and Joe Galloway gave us such a gift with their magnificent Vietnam history, *We Were Soldiers Once . . . and Young*.

Never the sort to rest on their laurels, that unlikely duo—a general and a reporter who stood and fought side by side in a terrible battle and became best friends—has now given us another gift with this story of their journey back to the remote Ia Drang battlefields, in company with the North Vietnamese Army commanders who fought against them.

Together these old enemies who were becoming new

friends walked the ground soaked with the blood of hundreds of Americans and thousands of North Vietnamese, each searching out places and nightmares etched in their hearts and minds.

Our professional Army is a small, tight-knit community and Hal Moore and Joe Galloway are quiet heroes within that community. Just how small is that world? Well, Hal Moore as a young major in the early 1950s taught infantry tactics to Cadet Norm Schwarzkopf at West Point. He persuaded me to select the Infantry as my branch of service, even as my father, a major general, urged me to choose the high-tech Ordnance Corps, telling me I would never make general as a mud-foot Infantryman.

In the summer of 1965 I was a newly promoted major and adviser to a South Vietnamese airborne brigade in the Central Highlands, marching my battered troops out of the Duc Co area across thirty-five miles of dangerous country. Along came a young reporter for United Press International named Galloway, who marched with us. He turned up again, a quarter century later, at my headquarters in Saudi Arabia on the eve of the Persian Gulf War. We spent a couple of days together as I visited American and allied forces on the eve of the war, and then I sent him out to ride with the 24th Infantry Division tanks on their 250-mile end run around the Iraqi divisions in Kuwait. In my estimation Galloway is the finest combat correspondent of our generation—a soldiers' reporter and a soldiers' friend.

We Are Soldiers Still is the ideal follow-up to Moore and Galloway's *We Were Soldiers Once . . . and Young*. Through their eyes, and half a dozen journeys back to Vietnam since the war, we see the evolution of that country and people as they find peace after a thousand years of war. And we see a surprising concern and tenderness for each other among men who once had done their best to kill each other. If those men, veterans of the bloodiest battles of the Vietnam War, can become friends and pray together for all who died on that ground on both sides, then the war really is over and we can all be at peace.

Gen. H. Norman Schwarzkopf, USA Ret.

PREFACE

It has been more than forty years since those nightmarish days of November 1965, when an understrength 450-man battalion of the 7th U.S. Cavalry launched an audacious helicopter air assault into the heart of enemy territory in the Ia Drang Valley.

Before it was over three more battalions would join us in a close-quarters, no-holds-barred fight to the death in two small clearings in the jungles of the Central Highlands of South Vietnam.

Two-hundred thirty-four young American soldiers perished in and around Landing Zones (LZ) X-Ray and Albany in the first major battle between the newly arrived Americans and North Vietnamese regulars sent down the Ho Chi Minh Trail in division strength. The North Vietnamese lost an estimated two thousand killed in the month of November in those battles and several others that preceded them.

It was the first such collision between two fine armies, and it would stand as the bloodiest of the entire ten-year war when the total American death toll of 305 killed in action that month in that place is considered.

Those of us who survived, miraculously, amidst so much death and dying all around never forgot those days and nights, even though some had served in World War II and Korea and some went on to serve two or three more tours in that long, bitter war and other wars that followed.

Some of us have lived long enough to see our sons and now our daughters—even our grandchildren—wear the uniform and carry the battle to other enemies in places like Panama, the Persian Gulf, Haiti, Afghanistan, and, yes, Iraq. This reminds us eerily of the conflict of our own youth in Vietnam.

With the publication in 1992 of *We Were Soldiers Once . . . and Young*, the stories of those battles, which had nearly vanished from the memory of most Americans, were recaptured. The release in 2002 of the movie *We Were Soldiers* brought yet more recognition of the courage and selfless sacrifice of so many Ia Drang soldiers on both sides.

All along our war and our battles remained fresh in our memories and our nightmares. We had a lot of unfinished business that could only be conducted on those long-ago battlefields. We had old ghosts, old demons that tugged at hearts and minds and sent some of our comrades in search of a name for what ailed us, and help dealing with that ailment.

Years after our battles and our return home the Veterans

Administration and its medical specialists put a name to a condition many Vietnam veterans experienced, posttraumatic stress disorder (PTSD), and began, belatedly, offering group therapy to help veterans deal with the condition.

Our old commander, then Lt. Col. Hal Moore, had vowed years before that one day we would go back to the Ia Drang, to those blood-soaked clearings in the Vietnamese jungles, and walk that ground and do our duty of confronting our demons and freeing the souls of all who had perished there. The general declared that he intended to spend the night there and he wouldn't listen to reason or the refusals of the victorious Vietnamese Communists who now controlled all of Vietnam, north and south.

So much has come to pass in all our lives in these four decades. Some who survived the worst that hand-to-hand combat threw at them have died, and we miss them terribly. Many would be surprised, thirty years later, to receive medals of valor for their actions in the Ia Drang. Two of our favorite people, helicopter pilots Maj. Bruce Crandall, a.k.a. Ancient Serpent Six, and Capt. Ed "Serpent 1 6" Freeman, waited even longer before they were decorated with our nation's highest award for bravery above and beyond the call of duty—the Medal of Honor. Freeman's came first, in 2001, then Crandall's in 2007. They joined Col. Walter J. "Joe" Marm, USA ret., who also earned his Medal of Honor in the Ia Drang but received it in 1966.

Life, as they say, went on day by day for all of us. We took the good with the bad and kept moving ahead, each in his own way, always with an inner understanding that we had already seen both the best and worst that men can do to other men, and that nothing—not even the passage of four decades—can fully erase those images.

Joe Galloway likes to say that every day he has lived since November 15, 1965, has been a bonus, a gift from God, and it is so for virtually all of us. Joe, who covered his last war in 2006 in the rocky deserts and narrow belts of green along the rivers of Iraq, finally put away his helmet and fatigues and retired to his home place in Refugio County, Texas. He had done four tours as a war correspondent in Vietnam between the beginning in 1965 and the end in 1975. In between and afterward Joe also covered the 1971 India-Pakistan War, the 1971 guerrilla uprising in Sri Lanka, Indonesia's invasion of Portuguese Timor, Operations Desert Shield and Desert Storm in the Persian Gulf, 1990–1991, the U.S. occupation of Haiti in 1995, and two tours in Iraq, in 2003 and 2005–2006.

Riding with the M1A1 Abrams tanks of the Army's 24th Division in the 250-mile charge across the western Iraq desert in the Gulf War, Joe remembers offering up a prayer: "Dear God, don't let there be another Ia Drang Valley waiting up ahead. I've already seen that and these young men and women don't need that experience."

During those years Joe watched and reported the changes occurring in America's military—the shift from a draftee Army to an all-volunteer force, the shift from training to fight a long guerrilla war to an Army armed and equipped and trained to fight tank wars against conventional enemies similarly armed. Then, with the invasion of Iraq in 2003, he saw that Army swiftly take down Saddam Hussein's army and government in a three-week blitzkrieg but prove utterly unprepared and untrained to fight the insurgency that arose to bloody the Americans with improvised explosive devices (IEDs) in the middle of a burgeoning civil war that has dragged on for five long years now.

In his long journey as a witness to war Joe never again saw combat so vicious and hand-to-hand—never again saw wholesale slaughter so intense—as that he witnessed, photographed, and fought in so long ago in the Ia Drang Valley. An interviewer recently asked him if he had learned anything from going to war for so long. Joe responded: "Yes. I learned how to cry." He added that he also learned that some events are so intense and immediate and life-changing that you cannot simply stand motionless; cannot remain a mere witness; cannot be a neutral observer. You will take a hand, lend a hand, stand up and get involved because you must.

Our old commander Hal Moore's vow that he would again, someday, return to walk the remote battlegrounds of the Ia Drang Valley and, yes, to spend one last night in that place the Vietnamese call the Forest of the Screaming Souls, came to pass on our third trip back to Vietnam a quarter century after America's long, bitter war there had ended. It is that story and more we tell in this book.

What all of us know in our hearts is that we are soldiers still. Some of us revisit the battlefield in nightmares. Some of us wear scars, visible and invisible, that mark us as changed men who walk unseen among our neighbors, who have never known what it is like to hold a dying boy in their arms and watch the life fade from his questioning eyes.

The world may now know something of the events that changed us, but thankfully most are spared the experiences that are ours and the burden that is the province of men who have killed other men at the bidding of political leaders more concerned with personal pride and national honor than with peace.

Yes, we *were* soldiers once, when we were young. Now that we are old we are soldiers still. We are soldiers who mourn for young men and women dying on other battlefields in other parts of our world four decades and more after our war ended so badly. A generation of political leaders who studiously avoided service in our generation's war seemingly learned nothing from that history and thus consign a new generation of soldiers to "preemptive" wars of choice, condemning them to carry their own memories of death and dying through their lives.

May God bless and keep all soldiers, young and old, and may that same God open the eyes of all political leaders to the truth that most wars are a confession of failure—the failure of diplomacy and negotiation and common sense and, in most cases, of leadership.

We who still dream of war in our troubled nights hope against hope for peace and its blessings for all.

WE ARE SOLDIERS STILL

ONE

Back to Our Battlefields

For us it was an irresistible urge that gnawed at us for nearly three decades—a need to return and walk the blood-drenched soil of the Ia Drang Valley of Vietnam, where two great armies clashed head-on in the first major battle of a war that lasted ten years and consumed the lives of 58,256 Americans and perhaps as many as 2 million Vietnamese.

Joe and I had tried twice before, in 1991 and again in 1992, to reach the Ia Drang during our research trips to Vietnam. The Vietnamese government officials in Hanoi had flatly refused permission for such a journey, uncertain whether we had some hidden agenda among the restive Montagnard tribal people in the Central Highlands where our battlefields were located. Or perhaps because our battlefields were located just five miles from the Cambodian border and Khmer Rouge guerrillas had been raiding across the border in that area, creating havoc in the thinly scattered villages near that border.

When we suggested on our 1992 visit that we might simply hire a car and set off south to visit the Ia Drang, our Foreign Ministry minder pointedly said if we left Hanoi on such a mission we would be "followed by a car full of people; not very nice people; and we won't be able to help you then." Only with the publication of Joe's cover article on the Ia Drang in *U.S. News & World Report* and the release of our book—both translated into Vietnamese and very carefully read in Hanoi—did the roadblocks fall in the fall of 1993.

We had proved by our writings that our only desire was to accurately report what had happened in the Ia Drang Valley, and we were just as interested in their version of this slice of history as we were in our own. Visit by visit, article by article, our hosts warmed to us personally and to our quest for the ground truth about battles that had deeply affected our lives and theirs.

There was another important factor: The world had changed. Communism had died in the Soviet Union and was being transformed in neighboring China. The rise of the Asian tigers—capitalist neighbors like Thailand, Malaysia, Singapore, and Indonesia, whose economies were booming—had not gone unnoticed by Hanoi. They were maneuvering to gain initial diplomatic recognition by Washington and were seeking foreign investment and most-favored-nation trade terms. This would not come for another year. Communism was alive in Vietnam but it was busy putting on a new face.

Now, in October 1993, a chartered Soviet-made Hind

helicopter was lifting off the runway at the old Camp Holloway airfield at Pleiku in the Central Highlands of Vietnam. The two Vietnamese civilian pilots confessed up front that they had no idea where, in that rugged plateau that butted up against the Cambodian border, the football-field-sized clearing code-named Landing Zone X-Ray was located. So Bruce Crandall, one of the most experienced pilots in Army Aviation, and I knelt in the narrow space between them in the cockpit, unfolded my old and detailed Army battle map, and, using Joe Galloway's even more ancient Boy Scout compass, pointed the way to the place where our nightmares were born.

In the back of the rattling old helicopter was an assemblage of American and North Vietnamese military men, old soldiers all, who were journeying together to a place where we had all done our very best to kill each other in one month of ambush and assault and set-piece battles in November 1965. It was here that the men of America's 1st Cavalry Division (Airmobile) and those of the 66th, 32nd, and 33rd regiments of the People's Army of Vietnam (PAVN) had tested each other in the crucible of combat. An estimated 3,000 to 5,000 North Vietnamese regulars had been killed or wounded. A total of 305 Americans had died and another 400-plus had been wounded in that time of testing. No one who fought there, on either side, talked seriously about who won and who lost. In such a slaughterhouse there are no winners, only survivors.

What had now brought this little group of survivors together to travel back to a painful shared history? It was, of all things, a book published a year earlier that opened long-closed doors and allowed us to make this needed journey. The book was *We Were Soldiers Once . . . and Young*, written by Joe and myself.

We were bound, in this thirty-five-mile flight, for the jungled mountain plateau near the Cambodian border where I had led my beloved troopers of the 1st Battalion 7th U.S. Cavalry in a helicopter air assault into a battle where we would be vastly outnumbered at times. That any of us survived is testimony to the fighting spirit of the great young Americans—the majority of them draftees—who, when their backs were to the wall, fought like lions and died bravely.

Had I commanded the men on the other side I would have said much the same thing of the North Vietnamese peasant boys drafted into their own army and sent south down the Ho Chi Minh Trail to intervene in the war raging in the southern half of the country. They, too, fought bravely and were not afraid to die in the storm of napalm, bombs, artillery shells, and machine-gun and rifle fire we brought down on them. Now their commander, Lt. Gen. Nguyen Huu An, and I were in the air, returning together to that ground hallowed by the sacrifices of our men. This time we came in peace, old enemies in the process of becoming new friends—something that would have been inconceivable just two years before.

These seminal battles that opened the waltz in Vietnam—which would stand as the bloodiest of the entire Vietnam War—had been largely forgotten in the long years of combat that followed before helicopters lifted the last Americans off the roofs in downtown Saigon in April 1975.

Joe, a war correspondent who had stood and fought beside us in Landing Zone X-Ray, and I had made two trips to Vietnam in search of the story of those who fought against us.

These trips resulted first in a cover article Joe wrote in *U.S. News & World Report* on October 29, 1990, on the twenty-fifth anniversary of our battles, and then in a contract to write our history of the battles. It was not lost on our former enemy commanders that we had dealt honestly with them and quoted them accurately in both the article and the book.

When ABC television and the *Day One* program offered to take us back to Vietnam to make a documentary film, the Vietnamese authorities in Hanoi agreed to all that we proposed, including the long-denied trip back to the battlefields in the Central Highlands.

Why this obsession with a remote clearing so far from anywhere? What had happened here years before that indelibly seared the experience into the minds and hearts of men who had fought in other battles and other wars? Those dark November days of 1965 still powerfully grip the imagination of those of us who survived the battles of the Ia Drang on both sides.

Late on Saturday, November 13 of that year, my undersized battalion of only 450 men—most of them draftees led by a hard corps of career Army sergeants who had fought as Infantrymen in Korea and World War II—was ordered to make an air assault by Huey helicopters deep into enemy-controlled territory just five miles from the Cambodian border.

The orders to me were simple: We believe there is a regiment (about 1,500 troops) of North Vietnamese Army (NVA) soldiers in the area of the Chu Pong Massif, a craggy spine of tumbled peaks over 2,300 feet high that ended at a clearing not far from the Drang River but reached back over ten miles into Cambodia. Take your battalion in there and find and kill them.

That evening I sat on a dirt wall at an old French fort near the Special Forces A-Team Camp at Plei Me village with Sgt. Maj. Basil L. Plumley, my right arm in this battalion. We had trained these soldiers for eighteen months at Fort Benning, Georgia, brought them to Vietnam on a troopship, and now we talked about what was coming.

My immediate boss, Col. Tim Brown, who commanded the 3rd Brigade of the Air Cavalry Division, had only twenty-one Huey helicopters assigned to him for this operation. He was giving me sixteen Hueys to ferry my 450 men into the wilderness at the base of the Chu Pong Massif. It would take at least five round-trips to get all my men on the ground; three hours or more, given the flight time to and from Plei Me Camp's dirt airstrip and time-outs for the helicopters to return to Camp Holloway in Pleiku to refuel.

The first lift or two would be extremely vulnerable if the intelligence was right and there was an enemy regiment in the neighborhood. The intelligence proved to be right in that regard, but it seriously understated the threat to us: There were *three* regiments of North Vietnamese scattered around our objective. We would be outnumbered twelve to one at times and our survival was by no means guaranteed.

On the early morning of Sunday, November 14, we scouted possible landing zones in the Chu Pong area, looking for clearings large enough to land at least six or eight troop-carrying helicopters at once. Our choices were very limited in that tangle of jungle and mountains. I settled on a football-field-sized clearing at the very base of the mountain, and gave it the code name Landing Zone X-Ray.

On that field and on another similar clearing two miles

away and closer to the Drang River, code-named Landing Zone Albany, the Vietnam War began in earnest. Over the next four days and nights 234 American soldiers perished in desperate hand-to-hand combat along with thousands of attacking North Vietnamese troops.

We set down on X-Ray at 10:48 a.m. in two waves of eight helicopters each. It would be at least thirty minutes before we would see those birds coming back with the second lift of my soldiers. Sgt. Maj. Basil L. Plumley and I were on the first chopper to set down on the field and we all jumped out with M16s and M60 machine guns blazing into the tall grass and scrub trees that encircled the clearing, just in case the enemy was waiting there for us.

They were not there, but they weren't far away up the slopes of the mountain. Within minutes we had captured a frightened North Vietnamese soldier hiding in a hole. He told us there were three battalions of the enemy on Chu Pong who wanted very badly to kill Americans but had not been able to find any—until now.

I gave orders to Capt. John Herren and his B Company troops to swiftly push out from the clearing so that any fighting would at least begin in the woods and, thus, I could protect the landing zone that was literally our lifeline. Only if we held that clearing could the helicopters return with more troops and more ammunition once the battle was joined.

Herren's men ran straight into clusters of North Vietnamese boiling down off the mountain charging straight into us. It was now 12:45 p.m. and the battle was under way.

Plumley and I moved around the clearing in the open as the din and rattle of gunfire steadily grew into a deafening roar. At times we could see the enemy soldiers maneuvering against us, and all in my little command group were firing back. After my S-2, or intelligence officer, Capt. Tom Metsker, was wounded in the shoulder, Plumley clapped me on the back and told me we needed to find cover right now: "If you go down, sir, we will all go down!"

We shifted quickly over to an old, eroded termite hill—the valley was dotted with these large Volkswagen-sized concrete-hard mounds of red dirt—and got it between us and the sizzling, popping, and deadly AK-47 rifle bullets the enemy was pouring on us like hot rain. In military jargon the termite hill became my command post, or CP, and here we would remain for much of the next three days and two nights as the fight raged all around us.

The second lift of helicopters brought in the rest of Herren's Bravo Company troops and a big chunk of Capt. Tony Nadal's Alpha Company soldiers. I ran out and ordered Nadal to deploy his men on the left of Herren's lines—and told him he had to secure a dry creek bed that came down off the mountain and directly into the side of the clearing. It was a natural highway for the North Vietnamese to come at us and I knew we had to hold it.

Not for the first time the thought crossed my mind that I was commanding a historic Army outfit, the 7th U.S. Cavalry, which had an illustrious and star-crossed past. This was a lineal descendant of the very unit Col. George Armstrong Custer led into another river valley, the Little Bighorn of Montana, nearly a century before with disastrous results. I was determined that what happened to Custer and his men was not going to happen to me and these modern-day Cavalrymen in the Ia Drang Valley.

I had something in my bag of tricks that Custer did not: the awesome firepower of initially two, and later four, full batteries of 105mm howitzers located in two clearings less than five miles away; clusters of rocket-firing helicopter gunships swarming overhead; and close-air support from Air Force, Navy, and Marine Corps fighter-bombers. The noise of battle soon was deafening and the thick smoke rising 5,000 feet into the sky marked clearly where we were and what was happening here.

Throughout an afternoon of pitched fighting—where acts of incredible heroism were common—the helicopters continued to come, bringing in the rest of my battalion and a reinforcing company, B Company of our sister battalion, the 2nd Battalion 7th Cavalry. The brave aviators set their Hueys down in that clearing under heavy fire and off-loaded fresh troops and more ammunition and water, and began ferrying out the growing number of our wounded. The dead, wrapped in their own green rubber ponchos, would have to wait. Their silent ranks, lined up near the command post, grew by the hour.

Just before dark I got a radio call from my operations officer, Capt. Greg "Matt" Dillon, who had spent the afternoon orbiting overhead in my command helicopter relaying our radio communications back to Brigade Headquarters in the Catecka Tea Plantation. Dillon told me when it was full dark he would be coming in with two helicopters loaded with ammunition and water and would bring with him the artillery and helicopter liaison officers.

He relayed an unusual request. ". . . Galloway wants to come in with us. Okay?" I had met Joe Galloway, a twenty-three-year-old war correspondent for United Press International, a few days before when we ran a long sweep operation searching for the enemy east of Plei Me Camp. He stayed with my companies day and night, not grabbing a helicopter back to the rear for hot chow and a shower. I liked that.

I told Dillon: If he's crazy enough to want to come in here, and you've got room, bring him. When they landed in the darkness I welcomed Joe to X-Ray and told him what we were up against. I noted that he carried a pistol on his belt and an M16 rifle on his shoulder, and looked like he could take care of himself in a fight. He was an unexpected reinforcement.

The fighting here raged on for two more days, until the afternoon of November 16, when the enemy suddenly evaporated and began their withdrawal toward sanctuary in Cambodia. Their commander left behind hundreds upon hundreds of his dead in a huge semicircle around us. We were ordered back to Camp Holloway outside Pleiku to rest and refit, and the helicopters began lifting out my men.

Joe walked over to say farewell to me. We stood and looked at each other and suddenly there were tears cutting through the red dirt on our faces. I choked out these words: "Go tell America what these brave men did here; tell them how their sons died." He did so. His stories and photographs of the battle at LZ X-Ray filled the front pages of newspapers around the world in coming days.

Around three-fifteen p.m. I stepped aboard a Huey piloted by Maj. Bruce Crandall, who commanded B Company 229th Assault Helicopter Battalion. I had flown in on Crandall's Huey and now I would fly out on it—the last man of my battalion to leave this bloody ground.

———

Behind us in the crowded, stinking clearing called X-Ray remained two other 1st Cavalry Division battalions that had marched into X-Ray earlier in the fight to strengthen our defenses: Lt. Col. Bob Tully's 2nd Battalion 5th Cavalry and Lt. Col. Bob McDade's 2nd Battalion 7th Cavalry.

That night Tully and McDade were alerted to march out of X-Ray the next morning, November 17, because headquarters had arranged for B-52 bombers from Guam to saturate the Chu Pong Massif with their huge payloads of 500-pound bombs. The target was too close to have any American troops within a mile and a half and they had to leave.

McDade was told to take his battalion to the clearing called Albany, two miles north, while Tully had orders to go to a landing zone called Columbus, two miles northeast, where two of the four artillery batteries that supported us day and night during our fight were located.

We might have thought the fighting was over, the enemy defeated and gone. But Lt. Col. Nguyen Huu An, the North Vietnamese commander on the ground, thought otherwise. He had a fresh reserve battalion, the 8th Battalion 66th Regiment, sitting in the jungle alongside the route to LZ Albany. They had missed out on the fight at X-Ray and were eager to get their turn at killing Americans.

Just after one p.m. the exhausted 2nd Battalion troopers were in a 600-yard-long narrow column that snaked through the high elephant grass and much denser forest near the Albany clearing. McDade had called a halt when his reconnaissance platoon captured two North Vietnamese scouts and saw a third escape into the jungle. He and his command group went forward to interrogate the prisoners, and McDade ordered forward the commanders of his other companies to receive instructions on how they would deploy as they marched into the clearing.

McDade's men dropped where they stood. They had been without sleep for four days and nights and the heat had taken a further toll. Men sat back on their packs, eating C rations, smoking, some falling into exhausted sleep. Alongside them, unseen in the thick brush and grass, the 8th Battalion and elements of the headquarters of the 33rd North Vietnamese Regiment deployed in a hasty L-shaped ambush.

The enemy announced their presence with a barrage of mortar shells and charged into the dozing American column with rifles blazing. Machine gunners and snipers hidden in the trees and atop the ever-present termite mounds opened up. It was every man for himself in a running gun battle that raged throughout the afternoon and, sporadically, throughout the night of November 17 and early morning of November 18.

At dawn the grim results became apparent: the shattered bodies of American and North Vietnamese soldiers were intermingled along the trail. Some bodies were in the trees, where artillery had blown them. Patches of blackened grass hid the bodies of soldiers of both sides who had been charred by napalm strikes.

The Americans had lost 151 men; another 130 were wounded. Four men were missing in action after the final tally, and their bodies were not recovered until April 1966, when I led the 3rd Brigade back into X-Ray and Albany.

One of the company commanders later wrote of that morning in LZ Albany: "It was a hell of a grim sight to see North Vietnamese and American bodies all over, intermingled. It was a hell of a fight; some North Vietnamese were bayoneted. It took the better part of 18 and 19 November to recover the dead and wounded."

Years later when Joe and I talked with the North Vietnamese commander, Lieutenant Colonel An, he revealed a keen memory of that terrible afternoon and night: "My commanders and soldiers reported there was very vicious fighting. I tell you frankly, your soldiers fought valiantly. They had no choice. It was hand-to-hand fighting. Afterward, when we policed the battlefield, when we picked up our wounded, the bodies of your men and our men were neck to neck, lying alongside each other. It was most fierce."

There was one last disastrous attempt to further bloody the Americans: Lieutenant Colonel An ordered another of his units to attack the twelve howitzers in Landing Zone Columbus, where Tully's battalion was waiting. The artillery gunners cranked down their cannon barrels and poured a storm of beehive rounds (shells filled with small razorlike pieces of metal) into the attackers. The enemy was beaten off with heavy losses.

That marked the end of what the Army would dub the Pleiku Campaign. By November 27 the last American units had returned to their base at An Khe on Route 19, some seventy-five miles away from the now empty battlefields of the Ia Drang.

In December I was promoted to colonel and assigned to command the 3rd Brigade of the 1st Cavalry Division. In the next eight months we fought the North Vietnamese and Viet Cong across the Central Highlands, from the South China Sea to the borders of Cambodia and Laos.

———

During that time I kept in close contact with Joe, alerting him when we were planning a new operation. Although Joe had seen war at its worst, he never shied away from one of my invitations to a new operation, a new battle: He marched with one or another of my battalions—usually his old friends in the 1st Battalion 7th Cavalry, especially those of Tony Nadal's Alpha Company—on most of my operations. Joe told me later that after the Ia Drang he believed he was bulletproof—after all, he came out of the battle without a scratch when so many all around him were killed or wounded. Only when he realized he was pushing his luck, taking foolish chances, did a healthy fear reassert itself.

Joe and I talked even then about the possibility that one day we would write a book about the Ia Drang. But we each had our careers, and as I moved up the ranks and Joe remained overseas doing three more tours in Vietnam and covering half a dozen other wars and revolutions for UPI, that plan remained on the back burner for both of us.

Late in 1976 Joe came through Washington, D.C., for briefings on his way to be the UPI bureau chief in Moscow in the Soviet Union. By now I was a three-star general and the deputy chief of staff for personnel (DCSPER) of the Army. We had dinner at my quarters at Fort Myer. After dinner that evening in November 1976, Joe and I shook hands and agreed that we would begin the research on the book as soon as I finished my Army career and he returned home after many years of foreign assignments.

Early one morning in January 1982, after Joe had finally come home to the job of UPI bureau chief in Los Angeles after sixteen years overseas, and I had retired from the Army and was living in Crested Butte, Colorado, Joe called and asked if I was ready to begin serious work on the book. He told me that the Vietnam War scenes in a movie (*American Graffiti II*) had triggered a frightening emotional response in him and he thought the best way to deal with the nightmares was to fulfill our obligation to tell the Ia Drang story. He said he had been sitting in his den in LA, arguably the safest place he had lived in many years, when that film caught his eye. Next thing he knew he was watching a mass air assault of 1st Cavalry Division troops in Vietnam, dozens of Huey helicopters disgorging Cavalry troopers, and enemy mortar shells exploding among them. "I was shaking like a leaf and crying like a baby," he told me. "I had no idea where that came from but sat up all night thinking about it. I knew if I tried to run from it it would catch me and eat me alive. So I decided to face it the only way I knew how: by fulfilling my promise."

Joe flew to Gunnison Airport and I drove him to my house on Mount Crested Butte on a cold, snowy winter day. The research began in earnest then and there. We wrote a questionnaire to send out to the dozen or so Ia Drang veterans we had addresses for, made some phone calls, and began the work. We had no idea that our chosen task would continue for nearly ten years.

Our big breakthrough came in August 1990. Joe was working for *U.S. News & World Report* magazine in their Washington, D.C., headquarters. He had proposed to his editor, John Walcott, that he return to Vietnam, with me in tow, to do research for a cover article on the forthcoming twenty-fifth anniversary of the now-forgotten Ia Drang battles.

During that trip, which ended on September 5, 1990, we met and interviewed Senior Gen. Vo Nguyen Giap and the historian of the Vietnamese People's Army, Maj. Gen. Hoang Phuong. We were also received by Prime Minister Do Muoi, Foreign Minister Nguyen Co Thach, and Vice Chairman of the State Planning Committee Le Xuan Trinh. We had moved heaven and earth in a failed attempt to get an interview with Senior Gen. Chu Huy Man, who had commanded the division in the Central Highlands in 1965. I sent a note and a bottle of Johnnie Walker Black Label scotch to General Man, asking to see him. He did not respond, but kept the whiskey. It is clear now that the Vietnamese were puzzled that a retired American general wanted to pursue the story of a battle he had fought and to meet the commanders who had fought against him. They were suspicious, and I believe the Defense Ministry in Hanoi advised General Man and General An to avoid us. During our time in Hanoi on that first trip we were housed in the Defense Ministry guesthouse just fifty yards from General Man's office. We were frustrated by the government's refusal to give us what we sought—interviews with my opposite numbers—while giving us access to everyone else.

We returned home and Joe wrote the story, which appeared as the cover article in the October 29, 1990, issue of *U.S. News & World Report*. America was poised to enter a new war, in the Persian Gulf, but had not yet dealt with how it felt about the last war—Vietnam. Joe's article touched a nerve and brought bags of mail to the magazine. Later it earned Joe and *U.S. News & World Report* its first National Magazine Award, the magazine world's equivalent of a Pulitzer Prize, in fifty years.

In the spring of 1991, after covering the Gulf War for the magazine, Joe was in New York for the luncheon where the National Magazine Awards were presented. He ran into Harry Evans, a former consulting editor of *U.S. News & World Report* and newly named president of Random House. Evans told Galloway: "I want that book." Joe responded: "What book?" Evans shot back: "The book you are going to write on the Ia Drang battles. I don't even need an outline. Your article is outline enough."

Fourteen months later, on November 11, 1992, Veterans Day, our book *We Were Soldiers Once . . . and Young* was published to critical acclaim, and it spent eighteen weeks on the *New York Times* best-seller list.

But the adventure wasn't over. It was only beginning. We returned to Vietnam half a dozen times in the decade that followed. We fulfilled our desire to walk the old battlefields and put some of our ghosts to rest. Not for nothing had the Vietnamese, after the battles, referred to the Ia Drang Valley as the Forest of the Screaming Souls.

We had to go there to mute their cries, even if we were the only ones who could still hear them after so many years. We had to go there because only we knew how and where they had fallen and how they died—filthy, sweaty, thirsty, caked in the red dirt of a foreign land—calling out to God, their mothers, their buddies.

TWO

Conversations with the Enemy

On the morning of the final day of battle in Landing Zone X-Ray, I stood looking down at the crumpled bodies of three North Vietnamese soldiers who fell, among many others, in a futile attempt to break through our lines. Dark bloodstains showed starkly against the yellowish uniforms, their limbs akimbo. I wondered who they were. Were they farm boys called by their country to serve, as so many of my own troopers were? What brought them here to this valley so far south of their homes to die on this battlefield? They seemed quite young, still in their teens. When my soldiers spoke harshly, with anger, of our enemies, I told them to remember that these men had mothers who would be shattered by the news of their deaths; that they, like us, had been caught up in great-power politics and were doing their duty as we were.

There were so many questions about the other side that lingered in our minds and, from the beginning of our decade-long research into the Ia Drang battles, Joe and I knew that somehow we had to persuade the North Vietnamese commanders to sit down with us and talk about how the battle looked from their side if we wanted the answers to our questions of why, and why there, in that remote valley. Although the prospects when we began serious work on our project that cold January day in 1982 seemed dim indeed, still we decided that when the time came we would make a strong push for this unprecedented opportunity to talk to our old enemies.

Not since the end of World War II in Europe had Americans been able to sit down with their former enemies and discuss in detail the battles they had fought—and it was possible then only because the German commanders were in our prisoner-of-war camps and had no real choice in the matter. No one likes to talk of their defeats, only their victories.

With that in mind, on the eve of our first return to Vietnam we bombarded the Vietnamese diplomatic mission at the United Nations in New York with requests to interview the North Vietnamese Army commanders who had fought against us in the Ia Drang Valley. We only knew the name of Senior Gen. Chu Huy Man, the overall commander, and Maj. Gen. Hoang Phuong, the historian who had written the North Vietnamese after-action report on the battles. The others who fought us—the battlefield commander, his battalion commanders and company commanders—were mysteries to us.

We met neither encouragement nor rejection from the

Vietnamese diplomats, but that first trip would prove both challenging and frustrating in the extreme.

At the time some of our friends and some of the veterans of the battles were astounded that we wanted to go back to Vietnam and sit down and talk to those men who had tried hard to kill us all—and we them—in the valley of death. For us, doing our best to record the truth of those battles for history, it was vital that we talk to everyone we could find who had firsthand knowledge, and that clearly included our old enemies.

The first of our many trips back to Vietnam came in August and September 1990, when we interviewed military and civilian officials in Hanoi for the *U.S. News & World Report* cover story on the twenty-fifth anniversary of the Ia Drang battles. Except for interviews with two remarkable Vietnamese officers, Senior Gen. Vo Nguyen Giap and General Phuong, our hope of talking to our actual opponents who fought us in the Ia Drang—and our stated goal of returning to the battlegrounds—failed to come to pass on that trip.

We returned again the following year, in October and November 1991, in the wake of the publication of Joe's prize-winning article, and things went a lot better. This time we were granted the crucial detailed interviews with the enemy commanders we had sought.

We tape-recorded hours of conversations with Senior Gen. Chu Huy Man, who as a brigadier general was the de facto division commander in the Central Highlands in 1965; with Lt. Gen. Nguyen Huu An, who as a senior lieutenant colonel and my opposite number directed the attempts to kill us all from a bunker on the slopes of the Chu Pong Massif; and with Major General Phuong, the official historian of the Vietnamese army, who as a lieutenant colonel was sent down the Ho Chi Minh Trail to write a lessons-learned report on the Pleiku Campaign. Their comments and answers to our questions were a vital part of our research.

As important as those 1991 interviews were, for us the real prize was our return in October 1993, when, finally, we were allowed to return to the old battlefields with Lieutenant General An and two other North Vietnamese veterans of the battles. Traveling with us was the ABC correspondent Forrest Sawyer and members of his documentary film crew, who captured it all for a one-hour documentary first broadcast in January 1994 on the now-defunct *Day One* program.

The last trip that Joe and I made together to Vietnam was in October 1999, when we visited the old French battlefield of Dien Bien Phu on a journey that grew out of a compulsion to see and walk that 1954 battleground that marked the end of a century and a half of French rule in Indochina and the beginning of America's equally doomed involvement in the affairs of the Vietnamese. General Giap told us that he felt if we Americans had studied carefully the lessons of the French and their defeat in Dien Bien Phu, surely we would never have gotten involved in Vietnam, and he urged us to visit and study the place where the Viet Minh under his command defeated the French.

Each of us has made one or two trips back to Vietnam without the other—Joe most recently in April 2005, when Vietnam was celebrating, in a curious fashion, the thirtieth anniversary of the fall of Saigon and South Vietnam.

As stated, the first trip back in 1990 was the most difficult both bureaucratically and emotionally. The tight-lipped Vietnamese indicated that we should fly to Bangkok and obtain our entry visas from their embassy. There we met our photographer, Tim Page, an Englishman and a legendary figure during the Vietnam War, if for no other reason than that he was shot or blown up by every party to the war—the U.S. Air Force, the Viet Cong, the South Vietnamese army, and the North Vietnamese Army.

Bureaucracies of every stripe are notorious for hating to have to confront a problem that has never been dealt with before, and upon our arrival at the Vietnamese embassy in Bangkok it was made amply clear that we were just such a problem.

They said they had no problem giving visas to Joe and Tim. They were journalists and journalists visited Vietnam frequently. But no American general had ever come back to Vietnam on anything but an official mission, and even then very infrequently. Why would I want to go back? What were my intentions?

Days went by as we waited for some official answer from Hanoi. The bills for our lodging and meals, paid for by *U.S. News & World Report*, were mounting as the Vietnamese embassy in Bangkok tried to get all the ministries—Defense, Interior, Foreign Affairs, as well as the Foreign Press Office—to sign off on letting us in.

Finally the press counselor in the embassy suggested we go see an Australian who lived in Bangkok—a businessman with very good ties to the highest levels of the government in Hanoi—who could better explain the problem. On a Sunday morning we sat down with the Australian in his luxurious home in the suburbs and over coffee he laid it out: Joe and Tim could go. I could not. Joe went ballistic and told the Australian that it was an outrage and a personal embarrassment to him, and if all three of us did not get visas then none of us was going to Hanoi. He asked the man to relay that message to his friends in Hanoi, and tell them that he would personally write every story about Vietnam for the next twenty years and they would not find it pleasant reading.

The Australian was aghast: "Surely you don't want me to tell them that?" Joe responded: "Surely I do, and in precisely those words." The phone rang at seven a.m. the next morning in Joe's hotel room. The press counselor informed him that visas for all three of us could be picked up immediately at the embassy.

We flew to Hanoi on August 28, 1990, and were met at the airport by Nguyen Cong Quang, the director of the Foreign Press Service, who arranged our appointments and assigned two excellent interpreters to us.

Quang told us that our request to visit the battlefields in the Central Highlands had been denied because of "security forces problems" in that touchy region along the Cambodian border. We pressed for an appointment with General Man both officially and privately, but got nowhere.

On August 30 we had a long session with a "Mr. Bai," who ran the North American Division in the Ministry of Foreign Affairs and later would be appointed Hanoi's ambassador to Canada. Bai was a hard man, clearly a veteran soldier and not a career diplomat. He told us he had fought the French and later commanded a prison camp for American and South Vietnamese POWs in the Mekong Delta. Among those in his charge was a U.S. Army major named Nicholas Rowe, who made a spectacular and successful escape from his bamboo prison, only to be killed years later by Communist assassins in the Philippines.

Bai told us that General Man was "out of town" and unavailable but he could arrange for General Giap to see us. He seemed bemused by our total focus on our war in Vietnam and suggested that we might profit from a visit to the Vietnam Historical Museum nearby. It was good advice, and during some slack time—waiting is a big part of any trip to the Far East—we toured the museum Bai wanted us to see. The high point for us was not the exhibits but finding a huge mural stretched across one long wall that was both a timeline and a map of Vietnam's unhappy history dating back well over a thousand years. There on the wall we saw thick red arrows dropping down into Vietnam from the north, depicting half a dozen invasions and occupations of Vietnam by neighboring China, and some of those occupations lasted hundreds of years before Vietnamese patriots and rebels drove them out, again and again and again. The Chinese section of the timeline stretched out for fifty feet or so. The section devoted to the French and their 150 years of colonial occupation was depicted in about twelve inches. The minuscule part that marked the U.S. war was only a couple of inches.

It put everything into a perspective few Westerners seemingly had ever considered before marching their soldiers off into the jungles of a nation full of ardent nationalists who had demonstrated that they were fully prepared to fight for generations until the foreign occupier got tired of war, or choked on his own blood. It was rich food for thought as we contemplated the political decisions that had brought my battalion to the shores of Vietnam and into pitched battle with a people who had no more give in them than the wild Scots-Irish frontier folk of Virginia and Tennessee and Kentucky and Texas who were always ready to shoulder a rifle and fight America's enemies when the time came.

We Americans had a strong taste of such warfare in the first century of our history. We, too, began with a revolution, an uprising against a distant and exploitative foreign colonial ruler. Then with the War of 1812 we had to again fight off the British, who invaded to recapture their lost colony. We fought Mexico in 1845 to settle the question of who owned what on our southern borders. Then we fought each other in the bloodiest war in our history to permanently weld a nation together as one people. To me it sounded like we had a lot of shared history with the Vietnamese people—except that their history was a thousand years and more of war and rebellion, while ours was only a couple of centuries or so. Our leaders would have done well to reflect on that before trying to pick up the mantle of the defeated French in Indochina.

Although we had bulled our way into Vietnam, it was becoming clear that the Vietnamese were going to have things their way: We were not going to get to interview the people we most wanted to interview or go to the one place we had to visit. Instead we were run through the typical round of courtesy calls on top government officials, just as any visiting foreign journalist would. Bai said the Vietnamese agenda was normalization of relations with the United States and a subsequent lifting of U.S. trade sanctions on Vietnam. He stressed that as far as the Vietnamese were concerned the war was over, a part of history, and it was time now to get down to normal business.

As if to underline the fact that it was their agenda, not ours, which would be pursued, they ran us through meetings with Prime Minister Do Muoi, Foreign Minister Nguyen Co Thach, and the Vice Chairman of the State Planning Commission, Le Xuan Trinh. We drank a lot of tea and listened to a lot of polite chitchat about their programs to entice foreign investment and diplomatic recognition by Washington.

The prime minister asked Joe to "take a message to President [George H. W.] Bush" that he hoped normalization of relations between the United States and Vietnam would come sooner rather than later. He promised that Vietnam would cooperate fully in resolving the cases of Americans missing in action from the war. Foreign Minister Thach also touched on the MIA issue, telling Joe that this was not just an American issue; that some 300,000 Vietnamese soldiers were also missing in the war. "My own uncle's son is missing in action. I understand the suffering of the American families," he said.

Normalization of relations between our two countries would wait for another president, Bill Clinton, and three more years; the debate was contentious and focused on demands for resolution of the MIA cases and Vietnam's record on human rights and its treatment of both Vietnamese and Montagnard tribespeople who had sided with America during the war.

Meanwhile, knowing what we had hoped to achieve by this visit, the Vietnamese were wasting our time and doubtless enjoying our visible impatience. All of it seemed familiar to Joe, recalling his own experiences living in Asia for a decade and more, and he told me of a Rudyard Kipling poem

he had engraved on a plaque that decorated his office wall
during those years:

> *The end of the fight is a tombstone white*
> *With the name of the late deceased,*
> *And an epitaph drear,*
> *A fool lies here*
> *Who tried to hustle the East.*

Our first significant interview on that 1990 visit was with
Major General Phuong, the chief of the army's Military History Institute for the past ten years. He met us at the Foreign
Press Service office. The general left a hospital bed to keep
his appointment with us, holding his right arm close to his
side, occasionally grimacing with pain from what he said
was a large swelling under his arm. Phuong was neatly but
simply dressed in a well-worn tunic and faded fatigue trousers
patched along one seam. He wore thick round spectacles and
had thinning, close-cropped hair. Phuong was cordial, knowl-
edgeable, and willing to share that knowledge.

Phuong told us that the People's Army had been studying
American tactics and weaponry since the first U.S. Marines
landed in Danang in March 1965; that they knew the time
would come when they would have to fight us. He said the
arrival of the 1st Cavalry Division (Airmobile) with its inventory of over 435 helicopters in the summer worried Communist commanders in the south. "We had to study how to fight
the Americans," he said. The general told us he had been sent
south, walking for two long months down the Ho Chi Minh
Trail, specifically to watch the Ia Drang campaign unfold and

to interview the North Vietnamese commanders and write an after-action and lessons-learned report for distribution to their soldiers.

Phuong told us that the NVA commanders planned to lay siege to the Plei Me Special Forces Camp to draw into an ambush a predictable South Vietnamese relief force. They anticipated that newly arriving troops of the 1st Cavalry Division would be sent in after that and then the Americans could be attacked and brought to battle. The historian said that with our helicopters we were very difficult for the NVA troops and commanders to deal with: "You jumped all over, like a frog, even into the rear area of our troops . . . you created disorder among our troops." He told us that the pressure from the Americans forced the Vietnamese retreating from the siege at Plei Me Camp to break down into ever smaller groups, until finally they were moving only by twos and threes like coveys of quail running ahead of the hunters.

Phuong told us, and showed us on my old Ia Drang battle map, that when the fighting began at Landing Zone X-Ray in the Ia Drang he was about three miles away from the battle-field. He said he could see the smoke and hear the artillery and air strikes. I asked if he then moved toward the fighting. He grinned and replied: "Oh no! I went in the opposite direction." Phuong told us that the North Vietnamese drew valuable lessons from the Ia Drang, lessons that they applied, with flexibility, throughout the rest of the war. Phuong's report, written in the immediacy of the moment after he had interviewed the surviving North Vietnamese commanders, was printed as a small pamphlet and quickly disseminated to the NVA and Viet Cong troops. It was titled simply: "How to Fight the Americans."

During our interview, he frequently referred to a small notebook that was filled with his handwritten account of his interviews with the North Vietnamese Army commanders in the fall of 1965. The notebook also contained meticulously hand-drawn maps of the battle areas. He seemed delighted by our intense interest in something he knew a great deal about, and was more than willing to share with fellow historians. We would have given a lot for a copy of his journal but had to settle for him reading to us from those pages covered with his notes.

The high point of our trip was our talk with General Giap, an architect along with Ho Chi Minh of the modern Vietnamese revolutionary movement in the 1930s. In the ensuing decades Giap built a formidable guerrilla army out of a mob of peasant farmers who answered the call to arms, and wielded that army with a brilliance and ruthlessness that helped pin down the Japanese occupiers in World War II, defeated the French, then the Americans, and even later the Chinese Communists when they briefly invaded Vietnam.

On September 2 we awaited his arrival at the front door of a formal government reception hall. Giap arrived in a small Russian-made Lada sedan accompanied by his aide, a burly army colonel. Giap, then seventy-nine years of age, was a small, slender man no more than five feet two inches tall. He wore a simple, well-worn brown army uniform with red shoulder tabs bearing four tiny gold stars. He had a kind face, sparkling eyes, and an open, friendly manner. There was nothing in his demeanor that spoke of a man who sent millions of his countrymen to their deaths in the wars of his lifetime. He appeared in good physical condition and moved swiftly and surely.

He shook my hand firmly and said: "I have heard about you during the war and I am glad to welcome you here, not as a commander of the 1st Air Cavalry but as a friend of the Vietnamese people." To Joe he remarked: "Your name I know as well. You are the war correspondent who carried a rifle like a soldier."

We moved into a large, twenty-by-thirty-foot air-conditioned reception hall. Giap and I sat side by side in two ornately carved chairs at the head of a large, low table, with Joe on our right and our interpreter, Le Tien, on our left. Giap's aide placed a tape recorder on the table and snapped it on. Joe did the same with our recorder. Giap did most of the talking, emphasizing his points with a strong, sure voice, using his hands and arms for emphasis. Several times he put his right hand on my left arm while making a point.

Giap made it clear that the Vietnamese people had been prepared to fight the Americans for however long it took to expel us from Vietnam, if it took ten years, or twenty years, or even longer. Over and over he emphasized that the Vietnamese were fighting for their freedom and independence; that we Americans were just the latest invaders and not the last, either. Giap told us that Vietnam's history contained the lessons that should have kept us out of there: "If the Pentagon had learned from the Dien Bien Phu battle perhaps they would have avoided going to war with us later."

The general, who was a schoolteacher before he joined Ho Chi Minh in the jungles to fight the Japanese, returned several times to lessons he thought the American commanders and political leaders should have learned, from Dien Bien Phu to the Ap Bac battle in the Mekong Delta in 1962, when American

———

helicopters were first employed, to the Tet Offensive. He said he loved to read, mainly history, and talked knowledgeably about George Ball's writings on Vietnam, and Neil Sheehan's *A Bright Shining Lie*. He groused about the difficulty of getting good books in Hanoi.

The general turned steely eyed when he spoke, with passion, of the relative strengths of the two warring nations: "You Americans were very strong in modern weapons, but we were strong in something else." He said we were the invader, the aggressor, while the North Vietnamese fought a "people's war, waged by the entire people," and they could fight everywhere or nowhere, and the choice was up to them. He expressed amazement that the Americans had no overriding strategy or goal in the war, only the tactics and weapons of a modern army and President Lyndon Johnson's declaration that we were not there to defeat North Vietnam, only to protect and preserve the South Vietnamese government. "Our goal was to win," Giap told us, leaving unsaid the fact that they did.

As our conversation with Giap came to an end, he inscribed and signed several books about him written in English that we had brought with us. He grumbled that some of them were less than accurate and one he dismissed as not only wrong but insulting. On impulse, I took off my wristwatch, an inexpensive Timex, and handed it to the general, telling him through the interpreter that it was a token of my appreciation—a gift from one old soldier to another. Giap held the watch in both his hands, looking at it with amazement, as tears gathered in his eyes and mine. Then he turned and clutched me to himself in a full embrace. It was my turn to be stunned as this former enemy—arguably one of the greatest military commanders of the twentieth century—held me like a son in his arms for a long moment.

We walked slowly together to the front steps and said our good-byes. His aide opened the door of the little khaki-colored Russian sedan and saw Giap comfortably seated before they drove off into the Hanoi traffic.

It would take another year and another trip to Hanoi before we finally got what we had wanted all along: the opportunity to sit down with the two senior commanders who had fought against us so long ago in the Ia Drang, Senior Gen. Chu Huy Man and Lt. Gen. Nguyen Huu An, both still on active duty, to my amazement. Both of these men had fought at Dien Bien Phu in 1954—Man as a division commander, An as a regimental commander—and were long past retirement age had they been American generals. In their army, officers down to the rank of colonel often remain on active service as long as they are physically capable. General Giap, now in his mid-nineties, is still considered on active duty even today.

In 1991, at the time of our meeting, Man was chief political commissar of the entire People's Army; his protégé, General An, was commandant of the Senior Military Academy, their version of our Army War College. At the time of the battles Man was a brigadier general commanding what was essentially a full division of North Vietnamese Army regulars from his headquarters near the Cambodian border, and An was a senior lieutenant colonel who commanded the troops fighting me from a command bunker on the slopes of the Chu Pong Massif.

Now, on November 4, 1991, at a reception room in the

Defense Ministry compound in Hanoi, a short walk from our now-familiar quarters in the shabby old guesthouse in that same compound, we came face-to-face with General Man, then seventy-eight years old, a member of the Communist Party Central Committee, chief political commissar of the People's Army, and one of only two generals Hanoi ever granted the rank of "senior general." Man was wearing a neatly tailored uniform with the four stars of his rank. He was about five feet three inches tall and of medium build. He brought to our meeting a printed map of the Central Highlands with details of the Pleiku Campaign and the Ia Drang battles clearly marked. Four other army officers accompanied Man, including the deputy commander of army archives and a lieutenant colonel from the army political department.

During the war we knew little, if any, details about the background of the enemy commanders we were fighting. The North Vietnamese commanders had grown up in a secretive system where nothing was revealed that might be of use to an enemy. Joe seized the opportunity to ask if Man would tell us about himself, share his biography with us. He readily agreed and told us some salient details of his life story. He was born in 1913 in the Central Highlands and joined the Indochina Communist Party in 1930, shortly after it was formed. He said he had been put in prison in Kontum by the French for revolutionary activities in the highlands not long after. The experience made him a committed lifelong revolutionary. Man said he had joined the Viet Minh army in 1945, and commanded a number of different regiments in the struggle against the French.

By the time of the pivotal battle at Dien Bien Phu, Man

had risen to become commander of the 316th Division. One of the regimental commanders in his division was a young major named Nguyen Huu An—and their careers would be intertwined from that point forward, from there to the Ia Drang and on through the entire war with the Americans. In 1975 in the final campaign against South Vietnam, Man told us, he commanded the attack on the port city of Danang from the south while his old friend and protégé, General An, attacked from the north. He said there were some 100,000 South Vietnamese soldiers in Danang at the time.

Man said that he was sent south in 1964, first to the coastal area of Central Vietnam; then to the Central Highlands; then, as commanding general of the Central Front, he organized attacks against the newly arrived U.S. Marines, including a fierce fight the Marines called Operation Starlight in the summer of 1965. From there he returned to the highlands to command the newly organized B-2 Front, a division-size command of some 30,000 troops, in what we call the Pleiku Campaign and the Vietnamese call the Tay Nguyen Campaign.

The general was very solicitous of our welfare, asking if we were being treated well and if our quarters were adequate. I told him both the accommodations and the atmosphere were a good deal better than they were in the Ia Drang Valley. Man laughed and replied: "We are sitting here on these chairs but we consider this a valley, too—a new valley."

Man told us that the original plan for the Central Highlands was to besiege Plei Me Special Forces Camp and lure a South Vietnamese army rescue column down Route 14, where it would be ambushed and wiped out. Then his forces would capture Pleiku and move down Highway 19 to the coast, effectively cutting South Vietnam in half. But with the arrival of U.S. Marines in Danang in the spring and later reports that a new experimental Air Cavalry Division, the 1st Cavalry Division, was being sent to Vietnam, Man said, that plan was put on hold in the late summer of 1965.

He told us, with a smile, that this plan was dusted off ten years later and parts of it put into effect in launching the final offensive that led to the fall of South Vietnam—launching the campaign with a surprise attack that took a key city in the Central Highlands, Ban Me Thuot, and began rolling up the South Vietnamese army and moving toward the eventual capture of Saigon. But in the fall of 1965 the revised plan was to besiege Plei Me Special Forces Camp as bait, destroy the inevitable South Vietnamese relief column, and wait for the newly arrived 1st Cavalry helicopter soldiers to get involved. "We used the plan to lure the tiger out of the mountain . . . I had confidence the Americans will use their helicopters to land in our rear, land in the Ia Drang area," Man told us. He said his command post was to the south of the Chu Pong Massif and LZ X-Ray and was subject to bombing by American B-52s that struck within a thousand yards of his position. He said the explosions left him temporarily unable to hear anything, but he recovered. Man said, however, that his troops were widely dispersed and very adept at digging in, and thus casualties from the big bombers were few.

Man told us that from his viewpoint the North Vietnamese won the Ia Drang battles. "Here we showed you very high spirit; very high determination. This is the first time we try our tactics: Grab them by the belt buckle! The closer we come to you the less your firepower is effective. After the Ia Drang battles we are sure we will win the limited war. We will destroy American strength and force them to withdraw."

The general deferred answers to our more detailed questions about the troop dispositions and tactics used at X-Ray and Albany to his old friend General An, who was the battlefield commander on the scene at the time. Before we left, General Man said in his opinion the meeting had been "open and friendly" and that augured well for better relations between our countries. He turned to Joe and added: "Also, today I got to meet a very famous reporter. I think your pen is stronger than my artillery. I hope your book will bring much better understanding to the American people and government. [They] can learn some lessons from your book on how to keep the peace."

Joe and I spent a sleepless night, he hunched over his computer transcribing the tape of our interview of General Man while I turned over in my mind all that had been said. What we got from the general was the larger picture, the thinking and strategy of a divisional commander and his superiors as they reacted to the arrival of American troops with high-tech weaponry, fleets of helicopters to ferry troops and supplies and even haul artillery pieces to remote battlefields. They struggled to find a way for a peasant army whose soldiers carried all their weapons, ammunition, and food on their backs—supplied by laborers who hauled 400-pound loads on bicycles down the Ho Chi Minh Trail—and moved swiftly through the jungled mountains by old-fashioned foot power to neutralize the American advantages. They had come to a simple but bloody way to level the playing field: Grab us by the belt buckle. Move in past the deadly rings of our artillery and napalm and 500-pound bombs and right into our positions. Then the American firepower is neutralized and the fighting is hand-to-hand, man-to-man, and nothing else matters but spirit and determination.

The next day we strolled back across the Defense Ministry courtyard, past the cage with the scruffy monkey sitting forlornly on his perch begging for peanuts and bananas, back to the same formal reception room, this time to meet the one man I wanted most of all to talk with: Lt. Gen. Nguyen Huu An, my opposite number, the man who directed the furious attacks against us at X-Ray and again at Albany from a camouflaged bunker on the slope of the Chu Pong Massif that towered above us. General An, a much taller and more robust officer than his old friend and mentor General Man, arrived with a rolled-up sketch map of the Ia Drang battlefields under his arm. He wore thick eyeglasses and his smile sparkled off a couple of gold teeth. After handshakes and introductions, An welcomed us with these words: "There's no hatred between our two peoples. Let the past bury the past. Now we look to the future. I am quite happy to see you coming to our country."

We spent over four hours closeted with General An and he had almost as many questions about our actions, orders, and plans as we did about his plans, orders, and thinking in the battles. One point worth noting: For all these twenty-six years since the fight, An thought it was my battalion, 1st Battalion 7th Cavalry, which he fought first in Landing Zone X-Ray and then "wiped out" in the ambush at Landing Zone Albany. He expressed total surprise when I told him that on November 16, 1965, the surviving 250 troops of my battalion were withdrawn by helicopter to Pleiku to rest and refit, and it was the 2nd Battalion 7th Cavalry that left X-Ray on the morning of November 17 on the fateful march to the Albany clearing two miles away. I was pleased that my withdrawal escaped his notice at the time because such maneuvers are fraught with danger in combat.

"Only today I learn that it was the Second Battalion; before I believed it was your battalion, General Moore," An told us. "I thought we finished your battalion off in Albany. I learn more details about this battle that I never knew. I think this battle on seventeen November [LZ Albany] was the most important battle of the whole campaign. Your soldiers were surprised when we attacked them but they fought valiantly. I tell you frankly your soldiers fought heroically; they had no choice. After the fighting when we policed the battlefield, when we picked up our wounded, I saw the bodies, yours and ours, neck to neck lying alongside each other. It was most fierce fighting."

Late on November 17, after X-Ray had been evacuated and abandoned, An said he was in his command post on the edge of Chu Pong Mountain. "It was a very rocky area. There were no trenches, no shelters. We could not dig through rocks. When I looked up at the sky I saw thirty-six B-52s. I counted them myself." He said the bombs from those B-52s struck half a mile to a mile away from his headquarters.

That same day, November 5, 1991, we had another long interview with Major General Phuong, the chief army historian. He provided the greatest detail on the battles at X-Ray and Albany of the three enemy generals we interviewed.

General Phuong had a detailed sketch map and again

———

brought his little green notebook filled with notes he had taken when he reached the Ia Drang battlefield on November 16, 1965. He told us that the surviving North Vietnamese commanders gathered after the fight and together they went over each action in the battles and the lessons that should be learned from them.

All three of the old enemy generals, who, like us, had spent much of their lives and careers in combat, emphasized that the greatest lesson to be learned from war is to cherish peace. They expressed their hopes that our research and writing would bring that lesson to the American people.

That night, after Joe had transcribed a long day of taped interviews, we lingered over warm scotches in dirty glasses and talked of all that we had heard that day in answer to the lingering questions we had about our battles. In this same old guesthouse, on our first visit a year earlier, we had talked about our fears that we would not be well received by either the enemy commanders we had come to interview or by the people of Hanoi, whose memories of America's Christmas bombing raids by B-52s in 1972 could not be pleasant ones. We were surprised by how warmly we had been welcomed then by ordinary people in the streets of Hanoi, and now by the men who had fought us in a historic battle. As we mused about this Joe said that in a strange way we were blood brothers to these men—that each of us had cared passionately enough about duty, honor, country, and our cause to kill and die. He voiced a final thought: In a world where most people couldn't care less how or whether you live or die perhaps we have much more in common with such men as these, our old enemies, men like ourselves.

THREE

You Killed My Battalion!

After being refused permission to journey to our old battle-fields in the Ia Drang on two previous visits to Vietnam, suddenly the official government objections on grounds of safety and security vanished.

Shortly after publication of *We Were Soldiers Once . . . and Young* in the fall of 1992, we were approached by a producer at ABC Television's *Day One* program. Terry Wrong told us he would like to make a documentary on the battles and the veterans that would involve taking a group of us back to Vietnam and to the battlefields.

After a series of studio interviews in New York, those chosen to make the trip to Vietnam included me, Joe Galloway, CSM (ret.) Basil Plumley, former A Company 1/7 Cavalry assistant machine gunner Bill Beck, former executive officer of A Company 2/7 Cavalry Lt. Larry Gwin, former helicopter commander Lt. Col. (ret.) Bruce Crandall, former A Company 1/5 Cavalry commander Lt. Col. (ret.) George Forrest, former C Company 2/7 Cavalry clerk Jack Smith, former A Company 1/7 Cavalry commander Col. (ret.) Tony Nadal, former B Company 1/7 Cavalry commander Col. (ret.) John Herren, and former B Company 1/7 Cavalry Sgt. Ernie Savage. Joining us would be the *Day One* crew: anchor Forrest Sawyer, producer Terry Wrong, interpreter Quyen Thai, and two crews, each with a cameraman and a soundman.

Before we left the United States for Hanoi, the Vietnamese government Foreign Press Office asked if there was anything else we wanted to do or anyone else we wanted to see on our trip. Joe immediately suggested that we ask that Senior Gen. Vo Nguyen Giap meet us at the Vietnam Military Museum in Hanoi and give us a briefing on his conduct of the campaign against the French at Dien Bien Phu. We sent a cable back asking for this.

We landed at Hanoi's airport on October 13, 1993, an hour behind schedule, and were met by our Vietnamese minders as we stepped off the plane. They were agitated and rushed us through the formalities in a matter of minutes. "General Giap is waiting for you at the museum," one of them explained.

It was clear that there had been major changes since our last two visits to Hanoi. The airport—still surrounded by the big water-filled craters that American bombs had dug in the rice paddies—had been expanded and was jam-packed with humanity, where just months before it had been smaller and much sleepier. Change did not end there. The highway to the capital had been widened, potholes had been repaired, and new homes and shops were being built along the roadside. Now there was real traffic to contend with on the highway and the streets of Hanoi—more cars and a plague of small, noisy, smoky motorbikes had joined the quiet stream of bicycles that had owned those streets before.

The death of Communism and the old Soviet Union had clearly had a salutary effect on a nation that had once been an important client state and the recipient of much Soviet assistance. That support had evaporated and Vietnam was now cautiously searching for another way forward that involved some of the benefits of capitalism, especially foreign investment.

The Vietnamese Communist Party, shaken but still very much in control, had decided to ease up and see what happened. After nearly four decades of rigid party control Hanoi residents were now experimenting big-time with capitalism and a more free market. A state-owned shop that once displayed four cans of evaporated milk in a dusty window had been transformed into the Hong Kong Kung Fu Video and Coffee Shop and its tiny tables were jammed with young Vietnamese watching Bruce Lee movies. On the sidewalk in front four new businesses were in operation selling trinkets, tea and cakes, tins of Russian caviar, and bottles of brandy. Change was in the air.

This ancient Red River Delta capital was bustling and busy where it had been quiet and somnolent on our previous two trips. A hundred privately owned restaurants had sprung up where once there had been fewer than half a dozen. People were building small brick and stucco two- and three-story shop houses alongside the airport road.

———

At the museum, with its welcoming array of gray-and-green-painted cannons, antiaircraft guns, and old Russian tanks, we were welcomed by a smiling General Giap. It was hard to square the image of this small, amiable gray-haired former schoolteacher with the fact that this was the man who, along with the former waiter Nguyen Ai Quoc, a.k.a. Ho Chi Minh, had built an army out of an unarmed gaggle of peasant boys and girls and led them with great skill against the Japanese, the French colonialists, the United States, and, more recently, against their former ally and neighbor, Communist China.

Giap greeted Joe and me as old friends in token of our two previous meetings and shook hands with the rest of our traveling squad during a brief stop in a museum reception room. He welcomed them as fellow soldiers to a Vietnam now at peace. Joe and I had talked through our feelings about these meetings with our old enemies on the earlier trips. For us this was research, capturing the words and thoughts of these men for history. Some of the others in our group of veterans were less comfortable with the idea; they were still angry at those who tried to kill them so long ago, and had in fact killed many of their friends. Some, like former-soldier-turned-journalist Jack Smith, expressed their feelings in the early discussions with the enemy commanders. Others listened quietly but tensely to the explanations of the North Vietnamese officers that their troops had no choice but to kill wounded Americans they found as they searched the battlefield at night for their own wounded and dead. How could we pass them by when they were still armed and might shoot us? asked one of the enemy generals. Most of the Americans would find peace on this journey.

We had asked for this briefing because of the importance of Dien Bien Phu and the defeat of the French in setting the stage for America's beginning involvement in the affairs of the two Vietnams. Giap had told us earlier that if we Americans had studied the lessons clear for all to see in the wake of Dien Bien Phu we would never have come here. He was right about that. Even more puzzling was the fact that we Americans had paid the tuition—by the end of the French war in Indochina the United States was financing about 70 percent of the cost of that war—but had not learned the right lessons. Any serious study of our war in Vietnam has to begin with the French war—and those were the books I read on the troopship that brought my battalion to South Vietnam in the summer of 1965.

Giap led the way to a large room in back where a huge twenty-by-thirty-foot sand-table exhibit depicted in full detail the battlefield of Dien Bien Phu, the scene of his greatest victory over the French in 1954.

The general, speaking through an interpreter, told us he made one daring decision that changed the course of the siege and history, a decision that he said could have cost him his life. After the French bet everything they owned in Indochina on drawing Giap and his Viet Minh army into a decisive battle in the remote mountain valley, Giap drew a tight cordon around their positions. Another army of peasant laborers pulled and pushed old American 105mm artillery pieces captured by the Chinese in Korea along a sixty-mile dirt road through the mountains.

His soldiers tunneled and trenched and burrowed in the red earth, drawing the noose ever tighter around the French strongpoints and positions, while the big howitzers were set into positions on the forward slopes of the mountains surrounding the doomed French garrison.

Giap was under orders from the Politburo to launch human wave attacks on the French in the late afternoon of January 26, 1954. He walked around the sand table with a pointer in hand, showing us all that had been made ready for the attack. But he said he had grown increasingly worried that such an attack would play into the hands of the French; that his artillery was vulnerable to the big guns of the French, and to launch human-wave attacks would destroy much of the force so carefully built and trained over the last ten years, with no hope of replacements for the terrible losses he would suffer in such an attack.

"I disobeyed my orders. I called off the attack," Giap told us. "At the time I wasn't sure if this would cost me my life." But Giap knew that he could not afford to use China's human wave tactics against the French because he couldn't replace either the manpower or the big guns sited in the open.

Instead he ordered his artillery pieces pulled back to the reverse slopes of the mountaintops, and the laborers began burrowing through the earth and rock to construct impregnable gun positions where they could fire on the French below and then swiftly pull the guns back into the mountain itself. His troops were ordered to keep digging the trenches ever nearer the French lines.

When everything was ready, then, and only then—on March 13, 1954—Giap signaled the attack, and this time he would use his tactics, designed for a Vietnamese army, first cutting French supply and reinforcement lines and the vital airstrip with his artillery while the Viet Minh troops closed in on and overran the surrounding French hilltop strongpoints one by one.

All this he told us quietly, matter-of-factly, with no hint of bragging or boasting. He was there; the Politburo was not. He knew the strengths and weaknesses of his army and the positions. He knew that the French commander was betting everything he had on a victory at Dien Bien Phu. So was he. It was a winner-take-all game and Vo Nguyen Giap would win using Vietnamese tactics, not Chinese tactics.

The men chosen to make this trip were all old friends and comrades. Nadal and Herren were both West Point graduates and professional Army officers. After retiring from the Army, Herren continued to work at the Pentagon as a civilian employee, while Nadal worked as a human resource officer in several large corporations. Gwin left the Army as a captain, earned a law degree at Yale, and practiced law in the Boston area. Forrest retired from the Army, coached basketball at his alma mater in Maryland for a time, and then became director of a program designed to keep disadvantaged minority youngsters in high school. Savage, after retiring from the Army, remained at Fort Benning, Georgia, as a civilian employee helping train Army Reserve soldiers. Beck, after completing his two-year tour as a draftee, went back to being a commercial artist. Crandall was badly injured in a helicopter crash on his second combat tour in Vietnam, and after retiring from the Army was public works manager in Mesa, Arizona. Plumley retired after thirty-two years in the Army, then worked as a civilian employee at Martin Army Hospital at Fort Benning for another fifteen years. Smith, after his two years as an Army draftee, went back to college and drifted into television news as an on-air correspondent for ABC, a job that his father, the broadcast pioneer Howard K. Smith, had held.

The following day our group of Ia Drang veterans met with Gen. Nguyen Huu An and seven of his commanders who had fought against us at X-Ray and Albany. The meeting was held outdoors on the shores of one of Hanoi's seven lakes. For most, on both sides, this was their first time to sit down across from each other. General An welcomed the Ia Drang veterans to Hanoi and did most of the talking on their side. I thanked them for the opportunity for such a historic visit by old enemies. The meeting outdoors in the sweltering heat was mercifully brief. We would have a chance to talk more that evening at dinner.

For all of us the greatest revelations and emotions came that evening at dinner on a floating restaurant built on a barge on Hanoi's West Lake. When we walked up the ramp we were stunned to be welcomed by a large table of Vietnamese war veterans who regularly gather there to talk of old times over a good meal. These were all crippled war veterans, men missing arms, legs, eyes. Their wheelchairs were crude and decrepit, as were the prosthetics replacing their missing arms and legs.

Any apprehensions we had at such a chance meeting of old enemies were quickly laid to rest as the Vietnamese veterans smiled and held up a hand-lettered sign that read, in English: Welcome American Veterans. Some of us blinked back tears. We shook hands warmly and visited with them for a few minutes before moving inside to a private room, where we were divided up and mixed together, Vietnamese and American veterans, table by table.

Joe and I were seated with the Vietnamese generals, Man,

An, and Phuong, whom we now felt we knew well from our previous trips and interviews. After a good Vietnamese meal of spring rolls, fish, chicken, and rice washed down by cold beers, we turned to the obligatory preliminary conversations about families and work and life in general as the hot tea was poured.

The lives of professional military officers are not all that different, no matter what country they soldier for. In our earlier interviews we had learned something about their families—General An had a daughter who was an army doctor and a major; General Man had a son who was an engineer and later would study in the United States; General Phuong lived with a daughter and her family. I had always urged my men never to celebrate the killing of an enemy—"remember that he has a mother too"—and to respect them as worthy opponents. From those same conversations and our book the generals knew something about our families as well.

There were the murmurs of a dozen other conversations at the small tables, the clatter of dishes in the nearby kitchen, which gave off the enticing scents of the next course. The lights of Hanoi sparkled around the dark lake.

Now the Vietnamese generals pulled closer to the table. General Phuong, the historian, spoke for them all. "We have had your book translated into Vietnamese and I have read it twice already and will read it again," Phuong told the two of us. "We like your book. You are the first serious historians to come here and ask us for our version of what happened and you quoted us accurately. You wrote that our soldiers fought and died bravely in battle, and for that we thank you. Like you, we love our soldiers."

The small, bespectacled Phuong—a lieutenant colonel when he arrived on the Ia Drang battlefields in 1965 to write the Vietnamese army's report and lessons learned on the battle and now a major general and chief historian of the Vietnamese army—had something else to say. "You wrote in your book that our men killed your wounded on the battle-field and this is true. But we want you to know that we never gave such orders. We always knew the value of prisoners. The situation on that ground was very difficult. The fighting was hand-to-hand and our wounded and your wounded were mixed together. Our soldiers could not go out in the dark and get our wounded and ignore yours, who were armed and could shoot them if they passed them by. These terrible things happen in the confusion of war, and not just on our side."

It was clear to us that our book about the battles had opened the hearts of these Vietnamese generals and it was that, and our determination to get and tell their side of the story as honestly as we could, that had opened the door to this journey back to our old battlefields.

Ours was not the only fascinating talk going on that eve-ning. Across the room at another table a stunning conversation was unfolding between a Vietnamese army colonel, machine gunner Bill Beck, and George Forrest. Through an interpreter the colonel asked where Bill had been during the fight at LZ X-Ray. Bill explained that he had been way out front, guard-ing the American flank next to the dry creek bed. He drew a quick map sketch on a paper napkin. George Forrest helpfully reached over and added the symbol for machine gun to Bill's X marking his position.

The Vietnamese officer gasped and turned pale: "You and your machine gun killed my battalion! Four hundred men.

You killed my best friend. I am godfather of his daughter and only last month I married her off. This is not very easy for me." Beck, whose memory of those terrible hours alone on that machine gun mowing down waves of attacking North Vietnamese is photographic and whose nightmares linger to this day, responded simply and quietly: "It isn't very easy for me either."

At other tables the Americans and Vietnamese told war stories and asked and answered the age-old question: Where were you that day? The dinner ended early since we had a 4:15 a.m. wake-up call to catch our flight from Hanoi south to Danang, where our road journey to the Central Highlands would begin. We headed back to our rooms at the sparkling new five-star Hotel Metropole with its modern amenities— such a contrast to our old quarters at the Defense Ministry with rats and huge spiders on our first two trips. It was quiet on the bus as each of us turned to his own thoughts about the dinner and our trip south to the Ia Drang in the morning.

FOUR

Traveling in Time

For our journey to the south and back to the battlefields in the Ia Drang we were joined by Lt. Gen. Nguyen Huu An, my opposite number as a senior lieutenant colonel in the X-Ray battle, and two longtime protégés of his who had also fought at X-Ray—Col. Vu Dinh Thuoc, who as a lieutenant had commanded a company in the battle, and Col. Tran Minh Hao, who had been an assistant regimental operations officer.

We flew to Danang, by the South China Sea, on a Vietnam Air jet, landing at the old American air base from which many of the U.S. air strikes against the north were launched between 1965 and 1972. Only the solid concrete revetments that once protected jet fighters against Viet Cong mortar and rocket attacks remained as evidence the Americans had ever been here. Our party got aboard four small minibuses at the airport and set out on a 200-mile drive south on Highway 1 toward the port city of Qui Nhon, where most of the Cavalry veterans first landed in Vietnam in mid-September 1965 aboard the troop carrier USMS *Maurice Rose* after a month-long sea journey from Charleston, South Carolina.

During our year in Vietnam the roads in South Vietnam had been subject to Viet Cong ambushes and the occasional mine dug in among the frequent potholes. They were dangerous and sparsely traveled by ordinary Vietnamese. Peace had brought much heavier traffic—trucks, buses, cars, motorbikes, bicycles, bullock carts, and foot traffic—to this main and only north-south artery. It had not, however, brought any widening of the two-lane asphalt highway and the potholes were still ever-present and bone-rattling. It was rice harvest time in this section of the country and the local farmers made use of the shoulder of the highway, and often parts of the highway itself, to spread out the harvested grain to dry in the hot sun. In the now-dry rice paddies along the road villagers were bent low, cutting the golden stalks of grain with small curved knives and stacking them. Women threshed the grains of rice from the sheaves with large wooden flails, then carried it to the road to spread it out to dry.

Dodging the rice and the people and the other traffic, especially the slow-moving oxcarts, made for a jolting, horn-honking, at times terrifying journey as our bus drivers negotiated the unending obstacle course through the broad coastal rice fields and on into the sand dune country where a once-sprawling American air base at Chu Lai had been taken apart, plowed under, and returned to the dry baking sand of the days before we arrived here.

We were now in Quang Ngai province, a poor, dry, sandy land more suited for cactus than palm trees. It was also well suited for revolutionaries. Quang Ngai and its people had been occupied by many armies, including ours, but never conquered. Its villages sent fathers and sons to fight the French and the Japanese and then us Americans. To see that the big air base the U.S. Marines had built here at Chu Lai had disappeared was stunning to Joe. He had accompanied the Marines who landed here in the summer of 1965 in an amphibious combat assault to seize and clear the territory for the air base. Now it was gone and it was as if it had never existed. Joe accompanied the Marines on many other combat operations in this area during his first seven months in Vietnam. He had many memories of this barren, sandy land and the sullen, hostile villagers who made it plain where their sympathies lay in this war.

Joe once told me of covering a large multibattalion Marine operation in Quang Ngai province not long after he arrived early in 1965. He and several other correspondents had worked their way forward until they were marching with the lead company at the point of the spear. There came one of those lengthy halts while commanders far to the rear debated what to do next. The Marines and the reporters pulled off the trail and settled in to wait on top of a nearby hill. In front of them was a broad rice paddy perhaps 200 yards wide. Suddenly a Marine sergeant shouted: "Look at that guy! Not one of us; must be one of you reporters." Down below a newly arrived reporter for the Associated Press, George Esper, trying to catch up, was halfway across the paddy and heading toward the tree line on the other side. Everyone shouted and hollered trying to stop him but George plowed on across the wet field and disappeared into the jungle, not realizing he was now the lead element of this operation. The Marines began saddling up to follow and rescue George or recover his body. Just then the reporter reappeared, leaping from the tree line back into the rice paddy and now running for his life. Behind him in hot pursuit was an old Vietnamese woman swinging a hoe, shouting insults, and doing her best to kill the foreign invader. George survived and covered the Vietnam War for ten long years.

Not far from the highway we could see a tall obelisk that, our interpreters told us, marked the site of My Lai village, where an out-of-control company of American infantrymen slaughtered some 400 women and children in the worst atrocity on our side in the Vietnam War. The worst single atrocity on the other side occurred north of here in the old imperial city of Hue during the Tet Offensive of 1968. A North Vietnamese division seized Hue at the outset of the offensive and, working from lists of targeted individuals, rounded up and executed more than 3,000 Vietnamese civilians whose jobs as local or regional government officials or schoolteachers cost them their lives. All of us who served honorably in Vietnam were unfairly tarred with the brush of the My Lai Massacre. That terrible event spoke more about a failure of American leadership than it did about the American soldier. I've always said that if that battalion's commander had been on the ground with his troops, instead of orbiting overhead at 3,000 feet in his command helicopter, the My Lai Massacre would never have happened. It also speaks volumes about failures in the training of both officers and soldiers at a time when the war machine was sucking up 20,000 draftees a month and the demand for sergeants and lieutenants was so great that people were awarded sergeant's stripes and lieutenant's gold bars who were hardly qualified and had not earned them. What a tragedy.

Every mile we drove south now brought us closer to the part of South Vietnam we knew best; the part where we soldiered in dozens of combat operations that reached from the South China Sea into the mountains of the Central Highlands. Soon we would reach villages and towns and the coastal plains with their rich, green rice paddies that we had known well. Places where we saw friends killed and wounded in a war that this land and these people absorbed and where they have now moved on as though all that never happened.

Our hosts were amused when we referred to the conflict as the Vietnam War. In their history books this small ten-year slice of time is called the American War. "Our people have fought many wars in the last thousand years. They are all Vietnam wars, so we must call them by different names to be more specific," one of the translators said.

Besides, he added, Vietnam today is a country, not a war. Before we finished this journey we would come to accept the truth in that statement.

In our stops for fuel or a bit of lunch over the next week of a road trip that would take us all the way south to Ho Chi Minh City, a.k.a. Saigon, we would get acquainted with Vietnam the country as well as Vietnam the war, trying to square our old memories with the reality of today, something the Vietnamese themselves seem to have done without regret.

Nearly two decades had passed since the last Americans were pulled off a rooftop by Marine helicopters in Saigon and South Vietnam fell to the Communists. The changes were evident and astonishing to those of us who had last seen these towns and villages in 1966. Over 65 percent of the people living here today had been born since the war ended, and the hordes of smiling, excited Vietnamese children who surrounded us to practice their English—a required course even in the smallest village schools—were testimony to the truth of the statistic. The end of war had clearly set off a baby boom of monumental proportions among these industrious, hard-working people.

The war so disrupted village life and rural rhythms that for most of that decade the United States shipped in millions of tons of rice to help feed the population. Today Vietnam is again one of the largest exporters of rice in the world. That population boom meant that the small, dirty towns and villages we remembered from combat operations long ago had grown like wildfire and now were large, dirty towns and villages bursting at the seams with people hustling to make a living. There were new schools for all those children, electric service in the unlikeliest of places, and a new form of entertainment that had spread across the land: billiard parlors. I'm talking *pool* here. Maybe only one table in a small thatch- or tin-roofed open-air pavilion with two shooters and a crowd of onlookers offering advice, but along Highway 1 most wide spots in the road had their pool hall.

Where the passion for pool came from was a mystery to

us. None of us remembered any pool tables in the clubs and recreation centers for American troops during the war, so clearly it was not an American legacy. Joe mused that during his years living in just-developing Asian countries like Indonesia where television had not yet arrived, the people were starved for any recreation at all. In Jakarta in the late 1960s promoters filled a soccer stadium with a huge crowd of ticket buyers to watch a local "strongman" do battle with a toothless and obviously drugged old African lion. Even when the strongman, the Great Lahardo, slapped the lion across the nose with a slab of raw meat, he couldn't get a reaction. The crowd was so incensed that it took platoons of soldiers to get the Great Lahardo out of the stadium alive. Some Vietnamese entrepreneur had seized on a similar hunger for amusement and somewhere to go in these little villages and introduced the locals to the game of pool.

The smells of this tropical country—simultaneously exotic, mysterious, and at times gross beyond description—are rooted in the memory of every American who ever did a tour here. All of them were still there to refresh that memory, from the smoke of charcoal cooking fires to unutterably foul gutters to ducks, pigs, and water buffalo living in backyards and along back alleys. Ah, yes, and there it is: the eye-watering, nose-twitching smell of nuoc mam, the fermented fish sauce so vital to any Vietnamese meal. Nuoc mam is prepared by filling small kegs with layers of whole fish separated by layers of salt. The kegs are left out in the sun for several months. The resulting juice is drained off the bottom. A little dab will do you.

As we made our way south we were surprised at just how little remained as evidence of the fact that over those ten years

3 million Americans served in the Indochina theater and billions of dollars were spent building bases and headquarters and housing and recreation facilities for those who came, did their twelve-month tour, and went home. Now they are gone. Far more remained to remind one of the French occupation of Vietnam and their last war with the Viet Minh rebels who rose against them in 1945 and, in 1954, defeated them. At the ends of bridges spanning the multitude of rivers and streams bisecting the highway small octagonal two- or three-man concrete Beau Geste forts with empty firing slits still stand silent guard with neither friend nor foe in sight. I suppose the old forts were built too well to easily tear down, and there's no market for concrete rubble.

But only the sharpest eyes could pick out the fragments of an American presence: a piece of perforated steel plate (PSP) among the bamboo and wire making up a farmer's fence around a cow or pig pen. Here a clattering, smoking truck whose chassis and engine once belonged to a U.S. Army deuce-and-a-half truck. There, in a small rural tea shop, a bulletin board whose notices were pinned up with individual flechettes, the modern-day equivalent of history's grape shot or canister rounds, small razor-sharp darts that once filled artillery shells fired by American artillery at enemy attacking at close range.

How could so many of us have fought here for so long and left so little behind in token of our passing except the Vietnamese military cemeteries that dot the countryside, north and south, each of them walled, neatly kept, and marked with an obelisk? Even as our own special teams scour the mountains and jungles of Vietnam for some 1,200-plus still-missing American servicemen, so, too, does the Vietnamese government search for the remains of over 300,000 of their own missing soldiers. Those they have found rest in the new cemeteries.

Even the huge piles of war junk we left behind—blown-up trucks and tanks, crashed aircraft, twisted steel runway plates—long ago disappeared into the holds of ships that carried it all away to Japanese steel smelters to be melted down and, doubtless, turned into Toyotas and Nissans for the American market. Or perhaps it has come back to Vietnam in the form of those noisy, smoky motorcycles that now clog the roads and streets. It is hard to believe that the American presence in Vietnam, which gave rise to huge bases that sprawled over thousands of acres, has simply been erased. We even built half a dozen creamery operations that produced white and chocolate milk and ice cream for the troops, and they too have vanished. Perhaps all of it was simply built on too large a scale and too flimsily, unlike those French forts, for the Vietnamese to consider worth keeping. All of it may be physically gone, but it is harder to erase from the memories of those who passed through.

Bruce Crandall says of this part of our journey: "I was amazed as we traveled south to see what an effort had been made to completely eliminate any sign of American wartime presence. It seemed unbelievable that they would not have used the buildings and infrastructure left by the U.S. forces. From Danang onward, I saw nothing American." Crandall added that we saw no sign of the Vietnamese having put to good use any of the equipment we had left behind—"no dozers, graders, cranes, trucks or other engineering equipment. I was told that all of this equipment was shipped out of the country to help pay some of Vietnam's war debt."

Nearing the end of this day's long trip, as we were passing through the Bong Son Plain—the scene of several major battles fought by my Cavalry brigade between January and May 1966—we stopped near the site of a temporary headquarters of my old brigade. It had been located near the end of a small dirt airstrip constructed by my Engineer troops. We had cleared this area of a tenacious enemy in some very costly battles during Operation Masher–White Wing. The enemy had been embedded here, as in Quang Ngai, for a long time among a people who believed in their cause. Afterward, when we handed over control to the South Vietnamese army troops, they flooded into the region with long-absent landlords and tax collectors trailing behind them trying to swiftly squeeze as much rent money and rice as possible out of the tenant farmers. Within a week of our departure the South Vietnamese troops and their locustlike camp followers were gone, too, and the enemy had returned and was back in control. It was here that I first realized the futility of this war. I climbed to the high ground and looked down on that overgrown and abandoned landing strip, which had been paved by some succeeding American commander. Again, nothing was left but the painful memories of brave men fighting and dying in a struggle for what?

After dark we pulled into Qui Nhon, the old port city where we first disembarked from the troopship in 1965, and checked in to a run-down hotel whose dark, dingy rooms offered plenty of mosquitoes and electricity that came and went according to some unknown and erratic schedule.

In the morning our little convoy took Route 19 toward the Central Highlands, and it was quickly apparent that the Vietnamese government had grasped both the strategic and economic value of that road. It had been turned into a four-lane superhighway minus the potholes and the chaotic traffic of Highway 1. We stopped at the top of the An Khe Pass, once garrisoned by 1st Cavalry Division units guarding against enemy attempts to cut off that chokepoint between the port below and the division base farther inland.

As we gazed across the rugged mountain slopes below, Bruce Crandall idly asked: "Didn't we lose a C-123 down there?" Larry Gwin, standing next to him, broke down sobbing. In an instant he was carried back to one of the worst days of his life, a day populated by the ghosts of war. That transport plane was carrying the mortar platoon of Gwin's outfit, A Company 2nd Battalion 7th Cavalry, from the base camp at An Khe to the Bong Son Plain for a new combat operation, Masher–White Wing, early in 1966, when it crashed near this pass with all aboard lost. That platoon was the only one from Gwin's company that had survived the fierce battle at LZ Albany in the Ia Drang with few casualties. It was then Lieutenant Gwin, executive officer of A Company, who was dispatched to this lovely, rugged mountain pass to attempt to identify the charred bodies of his friends, men he had trained with and fought beside. Now Bruce and Joe shielded their friend from the ABC crew's cameras and did their best to comfort him. It was neither the first nor the last time those of us on this journey would be ambushed by our memories.

After this trip Gwin would complete a book about his own memories of Vietnam, *Baptism*, which tells how his A

Company 2/7 Cavalry dwindled to only 15 of 110 original members of the outfit in just twelve months of combat. As this book was going to press in early 2008 Gwin had just completed writing a new post-Vietnam memoir: *The Imploding Man: Back Home from Vietnam.*

Our next stop was at An Khe, where we hoped to walk the ground of the division base camp we had hacked out of the jungle and scrub brush by hand with machetes immediately upon our arrival in Vietnam. That base was our home for a year, a huge sprawling collection of wood-floored tents sandbagged against enemy mortars for living quarters, rudimentary buildings that served as headquarters, even cruder buildings thrown up by each battalion as enlisted and officers clubs.

Standing at the entrance to the base area was a small Vietnamese army post with a scattering of stucco buildings and a gate with a surprised and nervous Vietnamese soldier carrying an AK-47 rifle. General An, wearing his uniform and badges of high rank, approached the sentry and told him we wanted to pass through and walk the old base. An told us this was now the headquarters of a reserve division of the army. The soldier told him he could not permit us to pass. Eventually he summoned an officer, a captain, who said there was no problem with us going around the new headquarters and onto the ground where our old base had stood, but he could not allow foreigners to enter through the post. General An's three stars seemed to carry less weight the farther we traveled from Hanoi—a phenomenon we would become better acquainted with in the days to come.

The buses could go no farther on the pitted and potholed

dirt track, so we hiked around the army headquarters, crawled through a barbed-wire fence, and walked out onto the plain and hills where once a mighty American division had roosted with its 435 helicopters and 15,000 soldiers. All of that was gone and what remained was farmland—rice paddies carved out of land cleared with American sweat and muscle, and on the edges where the land was poorer were hardscrabble patches of manioc and yam.

Sergeant Major Plumley and I walked to the spot where our battalion headquarters once stood. Again, no more than memories of nights spent writing letters to the families of soldiers who had died in battle and of days spent saying farewell to small groups of other, more fortunate soldiers who had survived a terrible ordeal and now were going home. This had been our home base during our year in Vietnam. Upon arrival a party had climbed Hong Kong Mountain, which loomed over the base, and there cleared a space, collected rocks, and painted them to form a large yellow 1st Cavalry Division patch with its emblematic black horse head. It was gone now, whether dismantled by some later American division or by the Vietnamese or by the mountain's relentlessly encroaching jungle I could not say.

I thought of how we spent the days here. I liked to rise early, in the coolness before dawn, and jog with some of my officers around the entire five-mile perimeter of the base, on a ring road of hard-packed red dirt just inside the tangles of barbed wire and machine-gun bunkers that guarded against an unseen enemy. It was quiet then, before the Army woke up, the silence only occasionally broken by the bark of an artillery tube firing a 105mm round. They called it H and I fire—

harassment and interdiction—shooting blindly into the distant jungle in hopes that it might blow up some hapless Viet Cong loping down an unseen trail. I don't think it worked very well, but we Americans had plenty of ammunition to waste. We learned to sleep through the steady booms of that friendly outgoing artillery addressed "To Whom It May Concern."

When I got back from my run I would wash up in a cold shower and then sit down with Plumley and discuss what our battalion had to do on this day. The routine—Did we have responsibility for manning the bunkers on a section of the line? How many men were absent, either sick with malaria or away on R and R for a week? When are our replacements arriving? Plans for the next operation, discipline problems, equipment needs. As we became more settled in this home away from home the amenities got a bit better. From three C-ration meals a day we progressed to two hot meals and one C ration. We all lived in Army tents, at first pitched on bare ground but later spiffed up with wood floors and sandbagged walls. Those floors were important when the tropical monsoon set in and the base turned into a sea of red mud, as opposed to the dry season, when we lived in a cloud of fine red dust stirred up by the endless parade of jeeps, trucks, troops, and helicopters coming and going. That fine red dust got into everything from our food to our laundry to our noses and mouths. The red mud, in its season, was even more maddening, as it stuck like glue to boots, fatigue uniforms, and jeep and truck wheels.

On our journey back in time, the 2nd Battalion veterans scouted around and found the site on a rock ledge looking out over the base camp where they had built a rudimentary shack and christened it the Garry Owen Officers Club. Men who fought hard and suffered much gathered here at night to drink hard and play hard. In the absence of any other entertainment they sang the old songs of soldiers at war as well as new songs they wrote to mark the battles they had fought. They rewrote songs written about George Armstrong Custer and the death of the 7th Cavalry in the Little Big Horn Valley to include a new and bloody valley of death called the Ia Drang. Someone even taped them one evening and I have a copy of that tape. You can hear the voices of men now dead and other men now old, as they were on a night in early 1966, when they were young men in their prime, engaged in a war their country's leaders thought was worth the sacrifice. Their beery voices on the tape are punctuated by the outgoing artillery rounds in the distance. Listening to the singing of Gwin, Rick Rescorla, Bud Alley, Jim Lawrence, and a dozen other young lieutenants and captains is like pulling back a curtain and peering back across forty-two years to a simpler, deadlier time.

After this march back through another place that now exists only in our memories we boarded the buses and continued up Route 19, again stopping briefly at the top of the Mang Yang Pass, where there is an old French cemetery with the headstones of hundreds of soldiers of Group Mobile 100, the French regiment that had fought alongside us in Korea, who were killed on June 15, 1954, when a Viet Minh ambush trapped their column in the narrow pass and slaughtered them in one of the final battles after Dien Bien Phu had fallen. This was the first place I came after we arrived in An Khe in the summer of 1965, to walk among those graves and take counsel of the sad lessons of the French war I had read about on the long boat ride to Vietnam. We were told the French dead were buried upright, their faces turned in the direction of home.

As we continued our ride toward Pleiku we could see small, neat concrete and stucco houses, each with its own garden, spaced out along either side of the highway. Those, we were told, were the homesteads granted to former soldiers resettled there when a People's Army division was demobilized in the Central Highlands. I suspect those new farmers were also the troops of that reserve division now headquartered in An Khe who, by their very presence, secured the strategic route into the highlands and provided a counterweight to the indigenous Montagnard tribal people, who, even today, have not come to terms with their new rulers.

I shared a seat on the bus with my old enemy, General An, and with a good interpreter at hand, we talked for hours of our lives and experiences in the service of our countries. An joined the Viet Minh guerrilla army in 1945 at age nineteen— the same year I was graduated from West Point and took up a second lieutenant's commission in the U.S. Army at twenty-three years of age. He commanded a regiment against the French in the siege of Dien Bien Phu and proudly told me that his troops captured the last strongpoint to fall, Eliane 2, before the French commander surrendered; he commanded two-plus regiments against the Cavalry in the Ia Drang; he was commander of the North Vietnamese division that blood-ied the 173rd Airborne and 4th Infantry Division at the Battle of Hill 875 (Dak To) two years after Ia Drang, and he led the division that was the first to enter Saigon in April 1975. After the end of our war, An fought in Cambodia against Hanoi's former allies the Khmer Rouge guerrillas. In 1979, An planned and led a daring, successful nighttime attack against Communist Chinese forces who had crossed into Vietnam and dug in atop a mountain. The Chinese had beaten back three previous attacks when An was urgently summoned from duties as commandant of the Vietnamese army war college and sent to the border with the mission of wiping out the Chinese and ending their punitive invasion of Vietnam. An told us he pulled back the Vietnamese troops to repeatedly rehearse the plan of attack, and when they attacked up the mountain the next time they overran the Chinese occupiers, killing or capturing all of them.

Virtually his entire life and military career had been spent at war, and Nguyen Huu An was every inch a soldier and a leader. This was our second meeting in two years and we were beginning to understand and like each other, and that bond would only grow stronger in the days ahead. I wondered then and still do at the vagaries of fate that pitted two such evenly matched military commanders against each other in battle. My respect for An was born on the battlefield before I even knew his name, and now it only grew as we became better acquainted sharing a seat on that bus.

While An was learning his trade fighting the French in those early years I was learning mine, first in the Army of Occupation in Japan and then on the battlefields of the Korean War. Between that war and the one where we met in battle I went through the usual variety of Army schools, tested experimental parachutes by the simple expedient of jumping out of airplanes while wearing them, and did staff duty in the Pentagon. Our experiences in very different armies were not all that different. We had more in common than a soldier of any army has with a civilian.

FIVE

The Backbone of the Army

Traveling in our group on the return to the battlefields was an old soldier who had been by my side every day of the twelve-plus months I served in Vietnam as battalion and brigade commander. Sgt. Maj. Basil L. Plumley was my strong right arm and had more time in combat, under fire, in three of America's wars than most soldiers have in the chow line. It was an honor and pleasure to find the good sergeant major standing beside me on this journey through old memories.

Through the years I have reflected often on the soldiers and sergeants with whom I have been privileged to serve in peacetime and in wartime. From the beginning at West Point I was taught that the soldiers were my responsibility; that their lives were literally in my hands. That is a heavy burden to place on the shoulders of a twenty-one- or twenty-two-year-old second lieutenant or a twenty-four- or twenty-five-year-old captain, and it simply could not be borne without the help and guidance of older, more experienced sergeants who are the mainstay of every outfit from platoon to division. They truly are the backbone of our Army and I thank God there were good ones, working with me, every day of my thirty-three years of service.

There was a sergeant, and a damned fine one, standing there when I stepped off the train on the first day when I arrived at West Point. There was a sergeant standing there when I took command of my first platoon in Occupied Japan. And another was waiting to help when I took over my first company as a brand-new captain in the middle of the Korean War. The best of them all, Plumley, was there beside me in bloody combat in the Vietnam War. Without them my learning curve would have been terribly steep and the price of my education paid for in the blood of many more American soldiers.

For a young officer in the American Army, selection to command soldiers in a line unit—platoon, company, battalion, brigade—is the very definition of success. There are many more hopeful candidates than there are command slots. The path up that pyramid is steep indeed, with each officer spending almost a year in advanced courses for his chosen branch—Infantry, Artillery, Engineering, Ordnance, Armor. The lucky ones get a shot at troop duty afterward but most are ordered to staff duty or teaching slots in ROTC courses or service schools. Then, as majors, some will make the cut and spend a year at the Army's Command and General Staff College. Again, the most fortunate will be promoted and assigned to command at battalion level, while the rest go back to staff duty at home or abroad.

As the officers shuffle along this route of advancement with its many transfers, who then assures continuity in the day-to-day running of the Army in the field? It is the non-commissioned officers, the sergeants, from squad leader to platoon sergeant to first sergeant, and, ultimately, the most experienced, best qualified, and carefully selected, the sergeants major. Officers come and go on their routes through schools and staff duty and command but the sergeants are always there with the soldiers—training, leading, and instilling and ensuring discipline.

I will never forget my arrival at the U.S. Military Academy at West Point, New York, on July 15, 1942. When my group of new soon-to-be cadets pulled into the train station we were met by a stone-faced, spit-shined sergeant with a pencil-thin mustache resplendent in Cavalry hat, Cavalry riding boots, and bloused riding breeches. His look implied that he had measured us, just as he had measured thousands like us before, and we did not for an instant impress him. His name fit him as well as those gleaming Cavalry riding boots: Master Sergeant Bonebrake. We fell into something like a formation and Bonebrake marched us up the hill and into the complex of imposing gray granite buildings brooding on the slopes and plain high above the Hudson River. There was a sense of age-less permanence, a majesty if you will, about that place, and a cold, powerful, unbending, relentless, no-nonsense authority. Master Sergeant Bonebrake fit in perfectly with the place and the weight of its history and those thick gray granite walls.

He was the first noncommissioned officer I met on Army

duty, and during the three long World War II years that followed that first meeting, Bonebrake would teach us the real art of soldiering—how to fire, clean, and care for the 105mm artillery piece and how to ride, jump, and care for U.S. Cavalry horses. By example he showed us how to look like and behave like a soldier, a dedicated leader, a man of authority and purpose. Through my own progression through the ranks and command of line units at every level from platoon (30 soldiers) to division (15,000 soldiers) there were always the sergeants there to help keep me out of trouble. I learned early to do a lot of listening when the sergeants talked, though I never lost sight of the fact that ultimately I alone was responsible for my unit's successes or failures.

When I took command of my Air Assault Battalion of 750 officers and men at Fort Benning, Georgia, in June 1964, it marked my first troop command since I had commanded a company in combat in Korea in 1952. On that day I met the most remarkable and memorable sergeant of a lifetime— Sergeant Major Plumley. He was the very essence of an Airborne soldier—six feet two inches tall, ramrod straight, lean, crew-cut hair, penetrating blue eyes, and a man of few words. Plumley judged men by their actions, not their words, and expected to be so judged by his own actions.

What struck me most on that first meeting were two small silver emblems worn above the serried ranks of colored ribbons on his chest: the Combat Infantry Badge with one star, signifying this man had served on the line in both World War II and Korea, and the Master Parachutist Badge with five combat jump stars in token of his participation in all four combat jumps of the 82nd Airborne Division in World War II and another one in Korea. I liked the man immediately and it turned out that we thought a lot alike when it came to soldiering and leading soldiers in training, in garrison, on maneuvers, and in battle. We could not know that early summer day in 1964, before the Vietnam War exploded, that we would be side by side for more than two years and, together with our battalion, would fight the first major battle of that war.

The sergeant major and I sat down with the battalion officers and I informed them that he worked for me alone and would take orders from me alone. Then he and I closed the door to my office and talked about our relationship and the battalion—its training status, discipline, the other NCOs, the officers, the morale of the troops, and the state of security of company arms and supply rooms. I told him he would have unlimited access to me anytime he felt it necessary, and that we would meet personally to talk at the beginning and end of each day of duty. He would oversee and improve the professionalism and promotion of NCOs in the battalion. When it came to punishment for disciplinary infractions by the troops or the junior NCOs I would always ask his recommendation.

As we launched an intensive schedule of training our battalion in the new and experimental art of air assault warfare—the movement of Infantry into battle by helicopter—Plumley was always there. He was quiet, laconic even, but on occasion he could be quite crusty and brusque. He was always candid and always all business. Where do we get such men? In the case of Basil Plumley, out of the hardscrabble hills of West Virginia, where he was born in the village of Bluejay on New Year's Day 1920, and where he came of age during the

Great Depression. He joined the U.S. Army in March 1942. Joe once asked him why he signed up. Plumley replied that it was "better than starving to death." He volunteered for paratroop training in August 1942—because, he told me, "I liked them jump boots." He probably also liked the $50 a month additional pay for airborne enlisted soldiers, too.

Assigned to the 82nd Airborne Division, Plumley made all four combat jumps of that unit in Europe in World War II: Sicily, Salerno, D-day at Normandy, and Market Garden in Holland. His World War II European theater service ribbon bears eight campaign stars and four invasion arrows. During the Korean War Plumley was a mortar squad leader with the 187th Airborne Regimental Combat Team and made his fifth combat jump at Sukchon, North Korea. His Korean service ribbon carries three campaign stars and one invasion arrow. By the time Plumley and I hooked up at Fort Benning he also wore a Silver Star for valor and three Purple Hearts awarded for wounds suffered in combat.

Between Korea and Vietnam the sergeant major rose slowly but steadily through the ranks and various assignments: platoon sergeant with the 11th Airborne Division in Germany, 1953–1956; first sergeant, rifle company, 3rd Infantry Division in Germany, 1956–1961; sergeant major, 23rd Infantry Battle Group, and 2nd Battalion 23rd Infantry, 2nd Infantry Division, Fort Benning, 1961–1964.

You won't find much, if anything, if you run the name of Plumley on Google or one of the other Web search engines. His response to questions about his life and service—even after the publication of *We Were Soldiers Once . . . and Young* and his memorable portrayal in the movie *We Were Soldiers* by the actor Sam Elliott made him a legendary figure—has always been: "I don't do interviews." Nothing Joe or I have told him about the importance of leaving his story, in his own words, for future generations of soldiers and sergeants has changed his mind about that.

What little we know of him is drawn from dry, official Army records and our personal exchanges during the years of our service together and our long, close friendship in the years that have followed. He is now eighty-eight years old and lives in comfortable retirement in Columbus, Georgia, just outside the gates of Fort Benning, with his wife, Deurice, the daughter of a West Virginia blacksmith. They have one daughter and one surviving granddaughter. A grandson died in a tragic auto accident shortly after completing an enlistment in the U.S. Air Force and just one week before we began filming the movie at Fort Benning.

Plumley was at my side as the first helicopter dropped us into the clearing we had dubbed Landing Zone X-Ray in the Ia Drang Valley on that hot morning of Sunday, November 14, 1965. He was beside me as the battle erupted all around us, and it was the sergeant major who grabbed my shoulder as the bullets buzzed and cracked around our heads like a swarm of bees in the first hour of battle at X-Ray and shouted over the noise: "Sir, you need to find some cover or you'll go down, and if you go down, sir, we will all go down!" When, on the night of November 15, during repeated enemy attacks against Bravo Company 2/7 Cavalry, an illumination flare tossed out of an Air Force C-123 plane circling overhead had a parachute failure and fell burning into a stack of ammunition crates near our command post, I saw Plumley calmly walk over, pull out the white-hot, still-burning magnesium flare with his bare hands, and throw it out into the clearing. For that, and other personal actions during those three days and two nights, I recommended Plumley for his second Silver Star for heroism in action.

It was on the second morning of the battle, with the enemy threatening to overrun and break through the thin lines of Charlie Company 1/7 Cavalry, that the sergeant major decided to begin rounding up some reserve firepower around our little command post. He walked over to Joe, who was lying flat as the bullets cracked past, thumped him in the ribs with the toe of his boot, and shouted down at him: "You can't take no pictures laying there on the ground, sonny!" Galloway got up, put away his cameras, unlimbered the M16 rifle he carried, and followed the sergeant major as he walked over to our makeshift medical aid station and spoke to the battalion surgeon and medical platoon sergeant. Plumley pulled his Army-issue .45-caliber pistol, jacked a round into the chamber, and declared: "Gentlemen, prepare to defend yourselves!" The battalion surgeon, Dr. Robert Carrera, who had been drafted into the Army out of his residency, looked at Plumley with shock and horror.

Plumley and I were side by side as we boarded the Huey helicopter piloted by Bruce Crandall, the last flight carrying the last few men of my battalion out of LZ X-Ray on the afternoon of November 16. A few weeks later I was selected for promotion to colonel and given command of the 3rd Brigade of the 1st Cavalry Division. There were two men I brought with me to my new command: Plumley and my operations officer, Capt. Gregory "Matt" Dillon. For the next eight months I made it a point to be on the ground with whichever of my battalions had the key mission or was in active combat on operation after operation, battle after battle, across the Central Highlands from the South China Sea to the borders of Cambodia and Laos. Plumley was always there every step of the way, working his magic on soldiers and sergeants alike, a calm and steady example of courage under fire.

In the late summer of 1966 we were both ordered back to new assignments in the United States and flew out of Saigon on the same chartered jet bound for San Francisco and on to Columbus, where our families awaited our return. After this tour Plumley was promoted to the new top rank among NCOs, command sergeant major. By now he wore the Combat Infantry Badge with two stars for his service in combat in three of America's greatest wars of the twentieth century. Fewer than 270 soldiers and officers throughout the Army survived the experience to wear that small silver badge of honor and courage. He served a second full tour in Vietnam, 1968–1969, as command sergeant major of the 2nd Corps advisory detachment in Pleiku, once again stationed in the Central Highlands. In 1972–1973, Plumley was command sergeant major of the 3rd Brigade 2nd Infantry Division and then 1st Corps command sergeant major, both jobs in South Korea.

In December 1974, I attended the retirement at Fort Benning of Command Sergeant Major Plumley and proudly pinned the Legion of Merit medal on my old friend's chest. Plumley had completed thirty-two years of active duty with the U.S. Army, but his service to our country and our Army was not at an end. He would work another fifteen years as a civilian employee at Martin Army Hospital at Fort Benning before retiring again to enjoy his bird dogs and quail hunting.

After my own retirement from the Army in 1977, my wife, Julie, and I spent most of each year at our home in Auburn, Alabama, a short forty-five-minute drive away from Columbus and Fort Benning. Julie and I were frequent visitors to the Plumley home, where Miss Deurice always had a fresh-baked pecan or sweet potato pie ready to cut.

In the late 1980s as we were researching the Ia Drang battles, Joe came to Auburn to do some work with me on our project. I drove him to Fort Benning to see where my battalion had lived and trained in 1964 and 1965, and then we headed to the Plumley home in Columbus for a scheduled visit with the sergeant major. Joe had not seen Plumley since our last field operation together in Vietnam in 1966. Plumley was standing patiently in his front yard waiting for us. Joe walked up to him and stuck out his hand. The sergeant major ignored that and instead pulled Joe into a bear hug, thumping him enthusiastically on the back. Joe's jaw dropped in total shock and surprise. "It was like I had been hugged by God Himself," Joe told me afterward. "I wasn't prepared for that."

Nothing speaks more loudly of the deep and lasting impression that Basil Plumley had on generations of young Army draftees than their reactions to his arrival at some of the first reunions of the Ia Drang veterans in the late 1980s. Although these men had served only a two-year obligation to the Army and nation and had returned to civilian life many years ago, as they gathered in the reunion hospitality suite a few would spot the old sergeant major in the door and, turning pale, would ease their way to the wall and try to make a stealthy exit behind him. Anyone who had ever been counseled for mistakes large or small by Plumley never forgot it and never wanted to repeat it. They were afraid he still had his old pocket notebook and that their names might still be written down in it for a long-delayed personal counseling session.

During these years Plumley gathered every Friday morning with a small group of other retired sergeants major at a local restaurant in Columbus for coffee and catching up on Army news and gossip. To the casual onlooker it may have looked like a typical group of old grandfathers at their usual table, laughing and joking and ragging each other over their coffee. But they are the lions in winter, the true backbones of our Army. Joe says that even though they wear PX plaid shirts these days he still sees, in his mind's eye, the rows of combat ribbons on their chests. For him and for me they *are* the history of America at war for half a century.

None of these old lions ever roared with greater effect than Basil Plumley, who has marched steadfastly through life adhering to the code of the hills of West Virginia, the rules and discipline of the Old Army, and his own sense of duty fulfilled and a job done well.

SIX

Back to the Ia Drang!

When we reached Pleiku in the Central Highlands, we discovered that the chartered helicopter that would take us to the Ia Drang battlefields would be delayed. Between that and the additional discovery that the green light given in Hanoi did not necessarily apply out in the hinterlands, we spent a nervous weekend in yet another shabby hotel. By now Joe had begun rating our lodging by his own variant of the star rating system—the rat rating system. He pronounced the Pleiku establishment a two-rat hotel, meaning each of us was guaranteed at least two rats in our room. He wasn't far off the mark.

Our old hotel sat on a dusty road in a poor section of Pleiku. The new wave of progress and construction had not made it to this wild west frontier town. A dozen or more Vietnamese schoolchildren had spotted the arriving foreign guests and now hung out in front of the hotel, pouncing on us when we emerged to gleefully practice the English they had learned in class. A snake charmer likewise swung into action when we stepped out the door.

It became obvious that the clearances from Hanoi and the presence of General An had their limitations here, just as they did at the Vietnamese army base in An Khe. Forrest Sawyer, Joe, and I began a round of calls on Pleiku Province People's Committee officials, who made it clear that no matter what Hanoi said there was only one clearance that mattered and it was theirs to bestow or withhold. Over endless cups of green tea we once again put our case for a historic return to the Ia Drang in company with General An and the two colonels. Having made his point, the chief of the province committee gave us his approval and we were cleared to fly on Monday, October 18.

In the meantime, worried about the delay in getting the chartered helicopter to Pleiku, I got clearance for Tony Nadal and one of our interpreters to drive out west and scout for an alternate way to reach the Ia Drang by jeep, truck, or even by foot if necessary. Tony came back and reported: "It was a trip from Hell." No doubt it was, but at least now we knew there was a way to get where we had to go if the helicopter failed to arrive.

On Monday we convoyed out to Pleiku Airport—formerly the old American airfield where once chartered jetliners and military transport aircraft jockeyed for ramp space and take-off and landing slots. Now it handles two Vietnam Air flights per week. None was due this day and we found the terminal locked and shuttered and deserted when we arrived. There had been a time when this place was buzzing like a hornets' nest, the roads jammed with Army jeeps and trucks, huge supply dumps packed with the arriving machinery of war, uniformed Americans moving purposefully in the tropical heat, big chartered jets unloading newly arrived soldiers to do their year in Hell, who marched past columns of smiling, fortunate soldiers who were going home. Now there was only silence.

Our group sat on the concrete walkway outside and a bull session with Colonel Thuoc developed. He told us he joined the Viet Minh army at age fifteen just in time to fight the French at Dien Bien Phu. He recounted how in September 1965 the company he commanded and others in the 7th Battalion 66th Regiment of the People's Army set out to march south down the Ho Chi Minh Trail through Laos and Cambodia bound for combat in South Vietnam. Each man carried in his pack a new uniform, packages of salt and rice, a plastic poncho/groundsheet, a packet of quinine tablets for malaria, and a personal notebook. The march took his unit two months and six days to the Ia Drang River, where they turned east into South Vietnam on November 10, 1965. Two days later they were told to change into the new uniforms they had in their packs.

The tall, thin Vietnamese colonel remarked that in 1965 his soldiers were well trained in all their weapons but had "very poor radios." He praised the U.S. Army's PRC-25 backpack field radio sets and, with a smile, said he captured two of the better American radio sets at LZ X-Ray. As the war continued Thuoc said his men captured enough PRC-25s and batteries to switch over to using them almost exclusively. Jack Smith, now an ABC national news correspondent, who in 1965 fought in the Ia Drang with C Company 2nd Battalion 7th Cavalry, asked Thuoc if his men had executed American prisoners of war during the battles. Thuoc replied simply: "Not intentionally."

The opening of Pleiku Airport terminal and the noisy arrival of the Soviet-made Hind helicopter that ABC was chartering at an hourly rate of $4,000 cut short the conversation with Thuoc as everyone scrambled to gather their packs, cameras, and water bottles. The white-painted helicopter normally flew for similar hourly pay for foreign companies exploring for oil offshore and for the U.S. Joint Task Force–MIA on its searches for the remains of missing American soldiers. It was not large enough to handle all of us, so we divided into two groups for the trip across the miles and years to Landing Zone X-Ray, some thirty-five miles and a quarter century away from Pleiku.

The two civilian Vietnamese pilots in the cockpit passed the word back to those of us on the first lift that they hadn't the foggiest idea where LZ X-Ray was located. The former Huey pilot Bruce Crandall and I moved forward and knelt between them in the cockpit. I showed them my old Army topographical map of the area and put my finger on the clearing. Not good enough. "Anyone have a compass?" we shouted to the rear. Joe fished around in his pack and pulled out a battered old compass he had carried as a Boy Scout. With it we oriented our pilots and, finally, were on our way.

For Bruce Crandall, squatting between the two Vietnamese helicopter pilots, the reasons for this journey were twofold.

"My purposes for going were to travel with my brothers back to the time and place where we first became a family, and to use the opportunity to find out everything I could about my missing helicopter and crew who are still missing in action," Crandall said.

Huey helicopter No. 63-8808 with crew members WO Jesse Phillips, WO Ken Stancil, Crew Chief Don Grella, and Gunner Jim Rice—all of whom flew missions during the Ia Drang battles—disappeared on a routine supply mission between An Khe and Qui Nhon on December 28, 1965. They were in Bruce's company in the 229th Assault Helicopters and the missing men have been on his mind for all these years.

Everywhere we went on this trip Bruce asked for information and help finding the crash site and the missing men. He said he was particularly grateful to Colonel Thuoc "for his assistance and continued efforts to find our MIA crew." The North Vietnamese colonel brought Bruce photos of downed Hueys from military files in Hanoi and at every stop on our journey questioned military and civilian authorities on the subject. "He was and is a true professional," Crandall said.

We watched out the windows and windshield as the city gave way to patchwork plots of small coffee and tea plantings, two or three small villages, and then we were over familiar territory—thick scrub jungle, meandering creeks, open areas with tall elephant grass and no evidence of human habitation. Much as it was twenty-eight years ago.

The first time I flew over this countryside was at dawn on Sunday, November 14, 1965, when we did an aerial reconnaissance mission searching for a clearing in the Ia Drang Valley suitable for our helicopter assault scheduled in just a few hours. To disguise our intentions the two Hueys and two escorting gunships flew a course from Plei Me Camp to Duc Co Camp on the other side of the Ia Drang River. Just passing by, but from the open doors of the helicopters we scanned the terrain carefully with binoculars. We needed a clearing big enough to take eight Hueys landing together. Only two clearings seemed large enough, one designated Yankee, the other dubbed X-Ray. Yankee turned out to have tree stumps dotting the clearing, so it would be X-Ray, at the base of the Chu Pong.

Now, from two miles out, Bruce and I spotted the X-Ray clearing dead ahead of us at the foot of the Chu Pong Massif. As we approached the clearing I saw clear signs that nature had done much to repair the devastation of war. Shattered trees had grown new branches. Shell holes and the line of old foxholes were at least partially filled. The elephant grass had reclaimed large swaths of land that had been burned over by fires set by napalm and bombs and artillery shells. I was stunned to see wildflowers blooming here and there in the clearing.

The helicopter settled to the ground almost precisely on the spot where Crandall landed that morning twenty-eight years ago carrying me, Sergeant Major Plumley, Capt. Tom Metsker, and my two radio operators.

The steps were lowered and at 11:15 a.m. I stepped down into the tall grass, closely followed by Joe and the sergeant major. For those of us who have known him for over four decades, Plumley's first name *is* Sergeant Major. He's that kind of man. Mrs. Plumley once cornered Joe at a reunion and asked him: "Joe, why don't you call the sergeant major

Basil? I do." Joe just shook his head and tried to explain to Mrs. Plumley why that would be unthinkable to him or any of us. "Ma'am, as far as I am concerned, his first name is Sergeant Major and always will be," Joe replied.

For years I had felt the need to return to this place and now, finally, I was here in the company of men who had fought both with me and against me. We were standing on the ground where so much had occurred that resonated throughout a war and throughout our lives. Each of us separated as we came off that Russian helicopter, each moving with little hesitation toward the places that were important to him. Our two nervous Vietnamese military intelligence minders warned us repeatedly of the dangers of unexploded shells and bombs and urged that we watch closely where we stepped. I felt certain that whatever higher power had brought us through this battle and other battles without a scratch had not brought us back here now just to see some of us die a delayed death from an old bomb or mortar shell. Our escorts weren't so sure.

We were met by a wall of oppressive heat and humidity as well as a fresh and unfamiliar green on trees and grass that none of us remembered from that November 1965. This time we arrived in the Ia Drang at the tail end of the monsoon season. The ground was moist and soft where in our memory it was baked hard as rock by the sun. Water flowed in what we knew as the dry creek bed—a tactically critical fold in the earth that both sides coveted and fought and died for during the battle. The trees now covered with fresh green leaves had been coated with red dust back then, and the bullets and shrapnel from bombs and artillery rounds denuded the trees of foliage in short order. We were instantly drenched in sweat and every movement was an effort. There was, with the departure of the helicopter, an eerie silence disturbed only occasionally by noises from the tall grass and the jungle forest: an unfamiliar bird's cry; the whir of insect wings; the distant chatter of a monkey. We heard none of that on our first visit here, when the thundering noise of bombs, rockets, machine guns, rifles, grenades, men shouting orders, other men screaming in pain and calling for the medic or their mothers shut out all other sounds and half deafened us. Then the only smells were smoke from the grass and trees set afire by our shells and bombs, the reek of cordite and gunpowder, the sickly copper smell of freshly spilled blood in large quantities, the awful choking odor of burning human flesh that once smelled is never forgotten. Then, as the days and nights wore on, there was the sickening sweet smell given off by hundreds of dead men bloating and putrefying where they had fallen in a large circle in the jungle all around us. There was none of that now. Only an occasional whiff of stagnant water the rains had left in the bottoms of old bomb craters and foxholes; a musty damp odor given off by the red earth itself; an exhalation of life and growth and greenery from jungle and forest. All around us the tall elephant grass was a brilliant green.

My former company commanders, Tony Nadal and John Herren, headed for the creek bed and beyond, where their companies had fought for three days and two nights. With them went Ernie Savage, now a retired master sergeant, who as a twenty-one-year-old buck sergeant in Herren's B Company had inherited command of the Lost Platoon after his lieutenant and two more senior sergeants had been killed in the first ten minutes of battle—and kept his men alive for twenty-seven hours while cut off and surrounded by a large force of North Vietnamese under orders from General An to wipe them out. They had to hike a hundred yards or more through the tall grass and scrub trees, with Major Hao the minder clucking over them like a mother hen as he warned them to watch every step they took. It wasn't the poisonous snakes that worried him. It was fields where unexploded bombs and mortar shells and 40mm M79 grenades had rested half buried and untouched for a quarter century but were still just as deadly as the day they rolled out of some American munitions plant. Hao wanted them to turn back, to abandon this risky trek, but they could not and would not. Eventually they came to that slight knoll where Savage had gathered the shattered platoon of twenty-nine men—nine dead, thirteen wounded, and seven able-bodied men—and fought off an enemy determined to wipe them out.

They found little that spoke of the twenty-seven hours that small, suffering little band spent cut off from the battalion, a tiny island of resistance in a sea of enemy soldiers who came at them over and over during the longest night any of them would ever know. Their medic, Doc Randy Lose of Biloxi, Mississippi, crawled from man to man plugging their wounds and his own with rolls of C-ration toilet paper after his bandages ran out, keeping them from screaming in pain when the morphine ran out and only silence and the black night was hiding them from the enemy all around them. When we pushed out during a lull in the fighting the next afternoon at first we couldn't find them. They had no time to dig foxholes, but during that night each of them had somehow burrowed down, scraping at the hard, dry soil with their fingers, and as

the artillery they called down on themselves and the encircl-
ing ring of enemies covered them with dirt and branches and
leaves, they became part of the earth itself. When we called
out for the twenty-one-year-old Sergeant Savage he slowly
raised his hand into the air and suddenly there they were in
front of us. From the time Savage assumed command of the
shattered platoon not another man was killed and Doc Lose
somehow kept all the wounded alive. They still had ammunition and were ready to fight on if necessary. Their story and
this place where it unfolded are legend in today's Army. When
we asked General An about this trapped platoon he shook his
head slowly and told us that he had ordered his troops to wipe
them out. "Their will to live was stronger than our desire to
kill them."

Bill Beck, a gifted artist who had sketched from memory
the places where he had fought not long after the battle, spun
around a time or two getting his bearings and then walked
straight to his old position, where, on his machine gun, he
had wiped out an entire battalion of North Vietnamese. Beck
had inherited the machine gun that first day of battle when
his gunner and best friend from back home in Pennsylvania,
Russell Adams, was shot in the head. Beck had vivid and dis-
turbing memories of running to Adams after he was hit, turning over his helmet and finding part of his friend's brain still
in it.

Standing there alone, Beck looked down and saw something unusual barely poking through the red dirt at his feet.
He scuffed at it with the toe of his boot and unearthed the
rusted remains of an American steel helmet. Just the top two
or three inches were intact. It was, Beck was certain, Russell

Adams's helmet. Beck scraped it out of the red earth with the toe of his boot, scooped it up, and slipped it into his pack. All this was done furtively and in a matter of seconds. Beck wanted no argument from the Vietnamese about him taking this relic that meant so much to him home.

Beck thought back to those days when he was Russell's assistant gunner. The two of them were from eastern Pennsylvania—Russell a small intense man of few words who came off his father's dairy farm outside Shoemakersville, and Bill a big, strong, six-foot-tall athlete who hailed from the gritty mill town of Steelton, just upriver from Harrisburg. They were so unlikely a pair that the guys called them Mutt and Jeff. When Russell took that enemy round in the head Bill was horrified. He ran over and scooped Russell into his arms, like a baby, and trotted across the dangerous open ground through a hailstorm of bullets to deliver his buddy to the medics, praying as he went—for Russell, for himself, for all of us.

It was nothing short of a miracle that he made it to the aid station and back, taking over the abandoned M60 machine gun just in time to halt an attacking enemy battalion in its tracks and hold them off for hours, out there alone on that crucial piece of ground. Bill and his machine gun saved my battalion from being overrun that day. In another, greater miracle Russell Adams survived his terrible head wound, emerging from an Army hospital many months later, disabled both mentally and physically—the wound left him partially paralyzed on his left side—and went home to the family dairy farm and back to the familiar hard work he had known all his life. Long after the war was over Joe and I went to the Army War College at Carlisle, Pennsylvania, and presided over an awards ceremony where Beck and Adams were each presented the Bronze Star with V for their heroism and sacrifice on this battleground. When Russell limped onto the stage—watched proudly by his wife and young daughter—he received a standing ovation and a hero's welcome from a military audience that wept openly. Our own tears were of joy at seeing our brothers honored by those who command a new and different U.S. Army and see men like Beck and Adams as an important part of their heritage and history.

Beck finding Adams's helmet was just the first of a series of magical moments that would transpire as we walked this ground.

Beck carefully snapped photos of the landmarks he had sketched a quarter century before—a termite hill where he saw an American GI on one side and a North Vietnamese soldier on the other, each hiding from the other. There was the gnarled tree where he had jumped to seek cover beside a sergeant during a burst of enemy fire and looked over to discover that the sergeant had a bullet hole in his forehead and was dead. All these landmarks where old, horrifying memories were lodged were still there. There was the creek bed where he saw a young lieutenant shot and killed while his radio operator, tethered to him by the long black cord of the radio handset, struggled to free himself but was shot in the back, his radio absorbing most of the damage. When he got home to Pennsylvania from this trip he cut the photos in half diagonally and did the same with copies of his old sketches, then married them up. They matched perfectly. Bill Beck had no false memories. The real ones, the totally scary ones, were engraved on his heart and lived in his nightmares and time had neither dimmed nor blurred them. They were razor sharp and still cut deep.

The only signs we saw of any human activity in this remote and wild area near the Cambodian border was a rough dirt logging road running east-west along the northern base of the Chu Pong Mountain with a rock-paved ford that took it across the creek bed. Two or three huge teak logs lay in the tall grass at one end of the X-Ray clearing. They looked like they had been there since the last dry season, waiting for the loggers to return and truck them out to the coast, where they would be shipped to Japan.

Fifteen minutes after we landed Plumley walked over to a large termite hill on the southeastern edge of the clearing. He had found our old command post, or so he thought. I walked over and immediately knew this was not where my command post had been located during the battle. For one thing, my CP was not on the southern side of the clearing near the mountain. It was actually on the northern side about 100 yards northwest of the sergeant major's termite hill. But by that time the false CP had become headquarters for this visit, a place of activity: people dropped their packs there, the TV crew was filming interviews there, and everyone scattered. So I said nothing and decided that I would walk over to the real location later when I could break away.

I was greatly moved to be standing once again on this ground where so much had happened that would shape and change the rest of my life and the lives of every man who fought here and survived against the odds. But all around me there was movement and shouts of discovery and the bustle and interruption of the ABC film crews, who were hustling to get their interviews with both the Americans and the Vietnamese. There was, at this moment, no time to linger over my own thoughts. Close by, General An—who was not a well man but had wanted to make this trip as much as I did—was standing through a long filmed interview by Sawyer and his crew. The burning sun was hard on him, hard on all of us, but Colonel Hao held an umbrella, lovingly shading his old boss.

As the day wore on I walked with Beck into the heavy growth where A and B companies had fought, where Beck had held the line alone with his machine gun, and down into the creek bed that before had been dry and sandy and where water now ran. I spotted a place where the grass was beaten down, marking where a large animal, likely one of the tigers who roamed this wild land, had bedded down. I also walked with Sergeant Savage and the film crew to the spot where his isolated platoon had held off dozens of enemy attacks in an epic struggle. Joe, Larry Gwin, and I walked the eastern side of the clearing hunting for traces of the line where C Company had held against a battalion of the enemy the second morning of battle, losing every officer and more than half the men killed or wounded. We found old eroded shell and bomb craters filled with water, and foxholes nearly erased by the passage of time. The foxholes were now no more than dimples in the earth, often with clumps of wildflowers blooming in them. I paused and thought how appropriate and peaceful a use nature had made of these violent intrusions of man and war. Twice we were forced to halt in the shade and rest to avoid heatstroke.

Then alone I walked down to the creek bed area along the old B Company position. There I came to a heavy stand of bamboo and nearby, stuck in the ground, was a five-foot-long, one-inch-thick bamboo stick sharpened on one end—just like it was waiting for me. I pulled it out of the ground and used it as a walking stick for the rest of the trip and brought it home with me.

The Vietnamese were taking no chances with our safety in this wild border area. A platoon of uniformed soldiers, complete with pith helmets and AK-47 rifles, came into X-Ray from their border post eight miles away and kept watch over our expedition throughout the day. Major Hao told us the Khmer Rouge guerrillas in Cambodia had raided as deep inside Vietnam as the town of Plei Me in recent years and were believed to shelter in the Chu Pong Massif that loomed over us at X-Ray, a craggy 2,000-feet-high mountain finger that ran the five miles west into Cambodia. The last large force of Khmer Rouge guerrillas still in the jungles did not surrender to the government of Cambodia until December 1998. Their cross-border raids into Vietnam clearly had our hosts quite worried about our journey into that region and our safety while there.

When Herren and Savage walked west out that logging road searching for the Lost Platoon position, the minders diverted them after a short distance. None of us was allowed to go more than a hundred yards or so in that direction. I was puzzled but believe I discovered why two years after our visit. An American veteran with business interests in Vietnam told me he had asked to visit X-Ray in 1995 and was driven there in a truck with an escort of two Vietnamese officers, one of them a brigadier general. He told me that, after visiting X-Ray, they drove a half mile or so to the northwest on that logging road and stopped near a crude timber archway. The two Vietnamese officers ordered him to remain in the truck and walked off down a path under the arch and were gone about twenty minutes. It was his theory, and one I accept, that the path led to perhaps the most remote, least-visited Vietnam Military Cemetery in the country and there rest the remains of thousands of Vietnamese soldiers who died in 1965 in the Ia Drang Valley battles.

Late in the day, as our time in this place was nearing an end, I called everyone together, Americans and Vietnamese, and we stood in a circle, arms around each other's shoulders, heads bowed. With one of the interpreters translating my remarks into Vietnamese, I said:

"Let us stand in silence, in prayer, in memory of the men on both sides, Vietnamese and American, who died on this ground, in this place, in November of 1965. May they rest in peace."

General An stood directly across from me in the circle, and when we broke he walked straight to me, his right hand extended. As we shook hands my old enemy pulled me to him and kissed me on both cheeks. Old enemies can become friends. I can't begin to explain the complexities of first impressions, but from our first handshake An and I hit it off. We had much in common as military men who had fought our country's wars, even though duty and orders pitted us against each other during one of those wars. We explored our common experiences as combat soldiers and commanders during the long hours on the van. Each of us had a reservoir of respect for the man who commanded on the other side in the X-Ray battle, long before we had a name and face for that unseen opponent. Although each of us had an inkling that he had outfoxed the other, outmaneuvered the other, we had come to understand with the passing of years that there were no victors in the battle—only the fortunate who had somehow survived so monumental a clash between two of the finest light infantry forces in the world.

Now it was time to leave. Our security troops had already marched off into the jungle, hoping to make it back to their post before nightfall. General An and his officers and our minder, Major Hao, and most of the American veterans got aboard the helicopter that would take them to Pleiku and then return to pick up the few of us who remained behind: myself, Joe, Larry Gwin, George Forrest, Forrest Sawyer, Terry Wrong, interpreter Vu Binh, and the two ABC film crews: Tom Levy and Bill MacMillan, and Minh Van Dang and Bruce Renwick.

As that Hind helicopter lifted off into a clear sky I turned to Joe and told him: "Tell the boys to go down to the creek and fill up our water bottles; then I want them to drag up a big pile of firewood." Joe looked at me like I was crazy, and asked, "Sir?" I responded: "Don't ask. Just tell them." He walked off toward the others, shaking his head.

SEVEN

A Night Alone on the Battlefield

As that Russian helicopter lifted off with seventeen Vietnamese and American members of our party, leaving only eleven of us behind, I thought back to a day in 1982 when Joe Galloway and I sat down at my house in the Colorado mountains and began planning the research for a book on the Ia Drang battles.

We talked over our battle plan and, near the end, we talked of what we wanted in this book that would be different. Joe said he wanted a chapter that would focus on the unseen and unheard victims of all wars—the families of soldiers who had died in battle who were the recipients of those terrible telegrams that begin: "The Secretary of the Army regrets . . ." I told him my dream was to return to Vietnam and to our old battleground; that I had to spend a night there and commune with the souls of my beloved men who had died there. Joe said it would be difficult for us to get back to Vietnam; unthinkable that the Vietnamese authorities would allow us into so sensitive a border area, and they would "never" let us spend the night there. I've seldom taken "no" or "never" for an answer.

That helicopter was coming back for us in forty-five minutes . . . or maybe not. My heart and my gut told me we wouldn't see it again till the next day. So I gave Joe my orders to relay to the stay-behind party. He gave me an astonished look, started to say something but thought better of it, and just nodded.

He walked over to the other nine, who were relaxing, enjoying a breather after a long, hard, hot day exploring the battlefield. "The old man says for you all to go down to the creek and fill our water bottles and canteens, and then drag up a big pile of firewood," Joe told them. They looked at him in amazement, and Gwin asked: "Joe, has the heat got to the Old Man?" Joe looked at him and responded precisely as he believed Plumley would: "Don't ask. Just do it."

Meanwhile, I concentrated on that helicopter not coming back. The sun was swiftly heading for the horizon. Darkness comes fast and early, around six p.m., this close to the equator. A few clouds were gathering out on that horizon as well, and I saw that as the harbinger, a message from God, if you will. There were many times when in my prayers I had asked the Almighty for just one night on my battlefield to commune with fallen comrades so that they and I could finally be at peace. Just one night, and now I was certain I was being granted that wish, that prayer.

As our party came back with the water bottles filled with creek water and popped in the iodine pills to make it safe to drink, and our woodpile grew to a respectable heap, I suggested that we pool what food we had, and that was collected in an empty cardboard box. I asked if anyone had a poncho to cover our woodpile. Joe grinned and slowly pulled out the only raingear anyone had thought to bring. Funny that it was the lifelong civilian among us who came equipped with the compass that guided our pilots here and now had the only poncho to keep our firewood dry, but Joe had done four tours in Vietnam and was a witness to half a dozen other wars and had learned his field skills the hard way.

The clouds were gathering into an ominous thunderhead now as we covered the woodpile and tucked our wallets and cameras and tape recorders into plastic bags. George Forrest sat down and, with Joe's Swiss Army knife, began shaving small slivers of wood into a pile of kindling that would also go under the poncho. All that could be done had been done and we sat back against the tree trunks and watched that lovely monsoon rain roar across the jungle and envelop us. There would be no helicopter flying back to get us tonight, I was certain. I would get my night alone on this sacred ground.

For an hour or so the torrential rains pounded us like so many jackasses caught in a hailstorm. Then the rain ended as quickly as it had begun. The sun was now gone and the darkness total. We were soaked and dripping but it was a good feeling, blessed relief from the broiling heat of the day. Before we could light our fire the sky above us cleared from horizon to horizon. We stood in silent awe as a brilliant panorama of blazing stars opened above us. There was no ambient light for miles in any direction; no streetlights; no well-lit homes; no distant glow of a big city; nothing to obscure the lights of heaven. Few of us in this modern time are ever blessed with such a sight.

Then an even more spectacular event began, as if on cue: a meteor shower. The bright blazing trails crossed the sky with a frequency and intensity that none of us had ever seen before. Hundreds and thousands of these shooting stars rained down on us here, where twenty-eight years before that same sky was lighted by tracer bullets, parachute flares, the bright white streaks of white phosphorus artillery rounds and the hot streaks of rocket-propelled grenades.

When this heavenly fireworks show finally slowed we lit our fire and gathered round it to dry our clothes. There was not only beauty in this place, on this night, but danger as well, and we talked of that. We had been warned there might be Khmer Rouge guerrillas sheltering in caves on the mountain looming over us, and during the day's explorations we had discovered in the ravine where the creek ran a place in the beaten-down grass where a large animal, likely an Asian tiger, had rested. I had also seen a colorful "two-step" viper moving through the brush—a snake so deadly it was said if one struck you it was maybe two more steps before you died.

Again we took an inventory. Our only weapon was Joe's pocketknife and our fire, which was both blessing and curse: its light might repel wild animals and snakes but it would also mark our position for anyone watching from the slopes above us. Beck sat down and began sharpening a point on a six-foot-long tree branch and then hardened it in the fire. With a good bit of laughter, we christened the crude weapon Beck's woolly mammoth spear. We had no radio communications link to Pleiku and no one suggested or even considered the possibility of a night march overland to what passed for civilization in this rugged, sparsely populated frontier. Here we were and here we would remain.

I lay down on the ground hoping to catch a nap, but sleep was elusive. Joe and Gwin sat close by listening to the night sounds of the jungle—the calls of frogs and gecko lizards, the hum of insects, the night songs of birds, the chattering and screams of monkeys, the roar of a distant tiger. I asked Joe if he had any of those Army-issue sleeping pills he had brought to combat jet lag. He dug out a plastic pillbox and found just one left, which he broke in half and shared with me. As he did so I heard Gwin sound off: "Men, we're in trouble now! The officers are doing drugs." Our laughter was added to the jungle's night concert.

Joe and Larry dropped off to sleep fitfully, but there would be little sleep for me this night, pill or no pill. There was too much going through my head; too many memories to take out and cherish in dark solitude. Alone, I walked away from the circle of firelight, and as my eyes adjusted to the night I found myself trooping the line of Charlie Company's old eroded foxholes on the southeast side of the clearing just inside the tree line. I had made this same walk on the night of November 14, 1965, asking how the troopers were doing. They were tired and thirsty but optimistic as always. "They won't get through us, Colonel," one responded. Another told me: "You can count on me, sir."

None of us knew then that the morning light would bring a two-battalion enemy attack against Charlie Company's thin line—600 or more of the enemy against 106 American officers and men. In just two and a half hours Charlie Company's five officers would all be either dead or wounded and only 49 of the 106 soldiers would survive unhurt. Even though two of the company's platoons were overrun by the attacking North Vietnamese, still they held the line against a formidable enemy in hand-to-hand combat. I was so proud of them. Now, again, I grieved for the brave young American soldiers who gave their lives for their buddies on this spot. I thought of the Charlie Company commander, Capt. Bob Edwards, radioing me that he was hit bad and directly under the sights of an enemy machine gunner but his men were still fighting. Bob had asked me for reinforcements but I knew they would only be shot up trying to move to his position. I had to tell him no; to just hang on and keep fighting. Then there was that bright young lieutenant, Jack Geoghegan, who had plans after the war to return to Africa, where he and his young wife, Barbara, had been missionary aid workers. Jack died here going to the rescue of one of his wounded soldiers, PFC Willie Godboldt. We found their bodies together where they had fallen. I had carried Geoghegan's lifeless body off this field in my own arms, thinking of his wife and their baby daughter, Camille, born just before we left Fort Benning. Their names, Geoghegan and Godboldt, are side by side, carved in the black granite of Panel 3-East of the Vietnam Memorial in Washington, D.C., among the 305 names of all the men who died in the Ia Drang. They are there together for as long as granite endures, a white officer and a black soldier joined in death by a bond that knows no prejudice, no artificial barriers. I thought of those words from the Bible that echo so strongly in the hearts of soldiers: Greater love hath no man than he lay down his life for the sake of another.

Then I turned and walked through the night to the termite hill where my command post, medical aid station, and ammunition and rations stockpiles had been located in a small copse of trees. Vivid memories of the combat that had raged all around, day and night, washed over me. Once again I sat down and leaned back against that old termite hill where my small command group had taken shelter from the enemy fire. It was here, on the second morning, that I looked up and saw two U.S. Air Force F-100 fighters diving right on us. The lead plane had already released two long cylindrical napalm canisters that were loblollying end over end directly toward us. I screamed at Lt. Charlie Hastings, the air forward observer, to call off that second plane before he dropped his napalm, too. Charlie screamed into his radio in the nick of time. In my mind I can still see those two cans of napalm pass just over our heads and explode, pouring flaming jellied gasoline over two of my engineer demolition troops in their foxholes twenty yards away. It set fire to some of our ammunition crates as well. Joe was sitting back against the termite hill with us that morning and I saw him jump to his feet and run out into that bullet-whipped clearing and into the burning grass to help rescue the horribly burned soldiers. That was the moment I knew in my heart that he was just as much a soldier as any man here.

What did all of this mean? Was all this suffering and dying worth it? Even then, in the dawn of this war that would drag on for ten long years and cost the lives of 58,256 Americans and millions of Vietnamese and Cambodians, our political leadership could not explain coherently why we were fighting halfway around the world against these people. It wasn't our place to question. We were soldiers and we followed their orders. In times and places like this, where the reasons for war are lacking, soldiers fight and die for each other. For the men on their right and left. Long after the war was over one president, Ronald Reagan, called it a "noble" effort. He was wrong. There's never been a noble war except in the history books and propaganda movies. It's a bloody, dirty, cruel, costly mistake in almost every case, as it was in this war that would end so badly. But the young soldiers can be and often are noble, selfless, and honorable. They don't fight for a flag or a president or mom and apple pie. When it comes down to it they fight and die for each other, and that is reason enough for them, and for me.

The strongest memory, and saddest, came back when I looked at a bare stretch of ground close by where the bodies of my men had been collected for the first leg of a long journey home to their loved ones. Each had been lovingly rolled into his own green rubber poncho by his buddies and then carried here. Only their worn black leather combat boots were visible, sticking out unnaturally from the covering poncho, the laces tied one last time a morning or two ago by their own hands. When I saw them so long ago I grieved silently, knowing a terrible truth that in a day or two or three telegrams would arrive at front doors all across America that would shatter the hearts and lives of their loved ones back home. I had no time to weep for them then but I have many times since. Here, on this ground, I wept one more time for seventy-nine men of my battalion who fell fighting in this place and would be forever young in my memory and those of their comrades and their families. I thought that the shower of meteors we had witnessed this evening was a gift to us, a heavenly tribute to the memory of all who died in this place.

I got up and slowly walked back to the fire. Gwin awoke and joined me, asking, "How're you doing?" I answered: "Fine. I'm just guarding the dead." As the hours wore on I would troop the lines around that clearing several more times. Joe later told me he woke up several times, raised his head, and saw me walking guard duty around the perimeter. He was comforted by the sight and would drift back to sleep. Sometime after three a.m. I heard a voice shouting from the jungle, echoing off the mountain slope. Two or three times that shout came: "Binh!" "Binh!" Everyone sat up, listening intently and wondering who was coming. Beck pulled his stone-age spear close. Our government interpreter, Vu Binh, yelled back, and into our clearing marched Major Hao and the platoon of Vietnamese soldiers who had stood guard over us the day before.

We learned from Hao that General An had been extremely concerned for our safety when the helicopter pilots refused to fly through the rainstorm and darkness to get us. He had tried to order the civilian pilots to make the dangerous flight and they flatly refused. The general then phoned the Defense Ministry in Hanoi in an attempt to force the issue. The alarm spread. An American general, two American journalists, two TV film crews, some American veterans, and a lone Vietnamese government translator had been stranded without protection in the jungle just five miles from the Cambodian border. Orders flowed downhill: If the helicopter can't safely do a night rescue then someone has to go overland to get them. Major Hao drove the thirty-plus miles from Pleiku to Duc Co town, on the other side of the river, commandeered an old Russian-made farm tractor, forded the river, and drove on to the border fort, where he collected the soldiers and began the march through a dark jungle toward X-Ray. Back in Pleiku our old enemy commander walked the floor all night long, worried about us.

We welcomed the rescue party and shared our food, water, and insect repellent with them. Then, one by one, we lay back down on the ground and drifted off to sleep. This time I joined them. I awoke at dawn to clear skies and walked the perimeter and visited my old CP alone, one last time, saying my good-byes to all the brave men who had perished here. Over by the fire George Forrest awoke, opened one eye, and there, standing over him, was a Vietnamese soldier in uniform and pith helmet, his AK-47 held at the ready across his chest. George told us later that in that moment he had a flashback to 1965 and feared he was about to be killed or taken prisoner. He measured the distance and calculated his chances of jumping and disabling or killing the "enemy" soldier and taking his rifle. Then reality sank in and he heaved a huge sigh of relief. This time the enemy was there to keep him from harm.

Not long afterward that Russian helicopter clattered in over the trees and dropped in to X-Ray. General An and his colonels and the rest of our party, including Plumley—who had done some worrying of his own over our situation during that long night—streamed off and greeted us warmly. General An wanted to call off the expedition then and there, canceling our plans to spend this day exploring Landing Zone Albany nearby. We argued strongly that we had come this far, without harm, and the mission should be completed. An reluctantly agreed.

As we gathered our packs and put out the fire I thought about the magical night we had spent here and what it meant. I was convinced that all who had died in this place were finally at peace and this place the Vietnamese now called the Forest of the Screaming Souls could at last be blessed with silence and we could go home with our own measure of peace as well.

EIGHT

Back to the Hell That Was Albany

Although the North Vietnamese commander, General An, had been up all night worrying about our safety and was very reluctant to continue this adventure, he finally gave the green light and we loaded back aboard the Russian helicopter for the short, two-minute flight from X-Ray to Landing Zone Albany. In our party there were three American veterans who had fought in that battle—Forrest, who as a captain commanded A Company 1st Battalion 5th Cavalry; Gwin, who as a first lieutenant was executive officer of A Company 2nd Battalion 7th Cavalry; and Jack Smith, a specialist four and company clerk of C Company 2nd Battalion 7th Cavalry.

The two and a half miles of terrain we had covered in a couple of minutes by helicopter had taken the long, strung-out column of weary American soldiers some four hours when they marched out of LZ X-Ray on the morning of November 17, 1965. They had not slept in three or four days and on their backs they carried the usual infantryman's load of sixty to seventy pounds of weapons, grenades, ammunition, three or four canteens of water, cans of C rations, personal belongings, and whatever "extras" they had been handed in the way of radio batteries, mortar shells, or spare ammo for the machine guns. The heat and humidity closed in on them, as did the scrub brush, tall elephant grass, and jungle through which they marched.

When the Recon Platoon at the head of the column reported the capture of two North Vietnamese soldiers—and the escape of a third who ran into the dense jungle—the battalion commander, Lt. Col. Robert McDade, moved up to personally interrogate the prisoners. He also, by radio, summoned all the company commanders forward to the head of the column to tell them how they were to deploy when their troops reached the big clearing dubbed Landing Zone Albany. The company commanders brought with them their first sergeants and radio operators.

The troops in that 600-yard-long column, now in triple canopy jungle, fell to the ground exhausted and took a welcome break. Some smoked, some ate, some leaned back on their packs and drifted off to sleep. At 1:20 p.m. the North Vietnamese, who had used the break to quietly maneuver a fresh battalion of the 66th Regiment plus elements of the 33rd NVA Regiment into position all down one side of the American column, launched their attack with a mortar barrage and then charged through the jungle into the Americans. Over the next eighteen hours there would be a ferocious gun battle, often at point-blank range, all along that column strung out over a third of a mile. The enemy had snipers up in the trees and machine gunners atop the termite hills. Before it was done and the surviving North Vietnamese withdrew the next morning, 151 Americans had died in the tall elephant grass, another 130 had been wounded, and 4 were missing in action.

Of such combat nightmares are born.

Because of the dense jungle it was not possible for our party to walk the full length of the Albany column. We were limited in our explorations to the clearing and the area that Larry Gwin identified as the battalion command post and aid station—yet another termite hill in a small copse of stunted trees whose trunks still wore the scars of bullets and shrapnel and napalm. The terrain in Albany, much closer to the Ia Drang River, was wetter and swampier than X-Ray had been. Whether because of the nature of the soil or the wetter conditions we weren't sure, but the foxholes and fighting positions we inspected at Albany were quite different from those at X-Ray. They had not eroded to the same extent and were easily recognizable for what they were. The corners were still square and the dirt on the parapets had not been overgrown. It was as if these old fighting holes at Albany had been dug a week ago or a month ago.

As Forrest Sawyer and his crews interviewed George Forrest and Larry Gwin, Jack Smith was shooting his own film with a small handheld camera for a half-hour personal program that would be aired on the *Nightline* program. All three of the Albany veterans were occasionally overcome by their emotions at this journey back to the scene of so much suffering and death.

———

On November 8, 2003, at one of our annual Ia Drang reunions in Washington, D.C., Jack—who had been diagnosed with terminal pancreatic cancer—was the featured speaker, and he talked of both the battle and his return with us to walk that field:

At one point in the awful afternoon at Albany as my battalion was being cut to pieces, a small group of enemy came upon me and, thinking I had been killed (I was covered in other people's blood), proceeded to use me as a sandbag for their machine gun. I pretended to be dead. I remember that the gunner had bony knees that pressed against my side. He didn't discover that I was alive because he was trembling more than I was. He was, like me, just a teenager.

The gunner began firing into the remnants of my company. My buddies began firing back with rifle grenades—M79s to those of you who know about them. I remember thinking: Oh, my God, if I stand up the North Vietnamese will kill me, and if I stay lying down my buddies will get me. Before I went completely mad, a volley of grenades exploded on top of me, killing the enemy boy and injuring me. It went on like this all day and much of the night. I was wounded twice and thought myself dead. My company suffered ninety-three percent casualties . . . ninety-three percent!

This sort of experience leaves scars. I had nightmares and for years afterward I was sour on life, by turns angry, cynical, and alienated. Then one day I woke up and saw the world as I believe it really is—a

*bright and warm place. I looked afresh at my scars
and marveled not at the frailty of human flesh but at
the indomitable strength of the human spirit. This is
the miracle of life.*

*Then . . . came an event which changed me: An
opportunity to go back to Vietnam. With ten other
Ia Drang veterans I traveled back to the jungle in the
Central Highlands and for several days walked the X-
Ray and Albany battlefields. What struck me was the
overwhelming peacefulness of the place, even in the
clearing where I fought. I broke down several times. I
wanted to bring back some shell casings—some physical manifestation of the battle—to lay at the foot of
the Wall here in Washington.*

*But search as I did I could not find any. The forces
of nature had simply erased it. And where once the
grass had been slippery with blood there were flowers
blooming in that place of death. So I pressed some and
brought them back. Flowers—that's all that I could
find in that jungle clearing that once held terror and
now held beauty. What I discovered with time and in
time may seem obvious, but it had really escaped me
all those years on my journey home from Vietnam and
my experience there: The war is over. It certainly is for
Vietnam and the Vietnamese. As I said on a* Nightline
*broadcast when I came back, This land is at peace,
and so should we be.*

*This has allowed me, on evenings like this, to step
forward and take pride in the service I gave my country. But never to forget what was and will always be*

*the worst day of my life: The day I escaped death in
the tall grass of the Ia Drang Valley.*

During his speech that evening Smith told the assembled
Ia Drang brotherhood: "You all should know that I was
recently diagnosed with advanced pancreatic cancer. If it is
from Agent Orange, which it may be, then it's not the first
time that damned war has tried to kill me."

Smith, the son of the pioneer radio and television broad-
caster Howard K. Smith, died a few months later, on April 7,
2004. He had found the peace that had eluded him for so
many years on our trip back to the Ia Drang.

Just how brutal and close the combat was in Albany is
nowhere better seen than in the story of Sgt. John Eade, a native
of Toledo, Ohio, who now lives in Boston. Back then Eade was a
squad leader in the 2nd Platoon of A Company 2nd Battalion 7th
Cavalry. Eade was one of a very few survivors of his platoon—
a horribly wounded man who staggered out of the jungle and
trees and into the Albany clearing the morning after the battle.
He was evacuated and, for four decades, had no contact with
any of the rest of us until Gwin found him. His story is pieced
together from his own account and a story written by the reporter
Jules Crittenden for the *Boston Herald* in November 2005.

Alpha Company was the only one of the line companies
to actually make it into the Albany clearing before the enemy
attack was launched. As company headquarters set up in the
copse of trees in the middle of the landing zone, 2nd Platoon
was ordered into the trees on the left side of the clearing and
the 1st Platoon swung right and into the trees on that side.
Few men of either group made it back alive.

———

Eade says his platoon was immediately pinned down when the enemy attacked, swarming over them through the trees and high grass. "For the first hour and a half it was intense hand-to-hand," he recalled. "It was like a gang fight . . . small groups of us versus small groups of them. It got down to knives. It got down to choking people." Eade said he and three of his men, Wilbert Johnson, Barry Burnite, and Oscar Barker Jr., were able to move and tried to flank the North Vietnamese. "We bit off more than we could chew," he said. Burnite was a machine gunner and Johnson, a black trooper, was his assistant gunner. When the machine gun was blown up and Burnite was hit in the chest with shrapnel in the same blast, Johnson dragged Burnite over thirty yards through the jungle in a futile attempt to save him.

Now it was Eade, Johnson, and Barker holed up and fighting among the trees. Johnson was killed and Eade was shot in the stomach and the right shoulder and a burst of shrapnel sprayed his legs and feet and a large piece penetrated one foot. He couldn't walk and was bleeding badly till Barker stuffed one of Eade's dirty socks in the hole in his shoulder. Eade was now firing his M16 rifle with his left hand. By three p.m. much of the fighting around them had subsided.

"I knew and he knew that everyone else was dead," Eade said. He urged Barker to try to save himself; to run across the fifty yards of open ground between them and the command post. "He refused to go." Not long after that Barker was shot in the chest and Eade had to watch him die a long, slow death. Eade was now alone. He could have played dead but that was not his way. "Playing dead was a way to die. It made no sense to me. Our job was to hold that position and kill the enemy."

———

In the command post they could see large groups of North Vietnamese moving through the 2nd Platoon area. The few survivors who had made it out told the officers they didn't think anyone was alive there. They called a napalm strike on Eade's area. He says it was the right decision even though it set him on fire. "I managed to roll in the dirt and put it out." With all his other problems, Eade said, being set on fire was inconsequential. Besides, the napalm served a purpose. "It flushed them out and gave me an opportunity to reduce the numbers," Eade added.

Late that day Eade was surprised by the sudden appearance of three enemy soldiers behind him. "There were three North Vietnamese looking at me, one with a pistol." He shot and killed two of them, but the one with the pistol shot him in the face, destroying his right eye socket and shattering parts of his sinus. The bullet knocked Eade unconscious. When he came to the Vietnamese with the pistol was gone and it was dark. Parties of North Vietnamese moved through his area until midnight, collecting their dead and wounded. Eade couldn't use his rifle for fear of giving away his position, but he collected up grenades from the bodies of his fallen comrades and used them on the enemy.

The middle of the morning on November 18, 1965, Eade heard rustling in the brush and prepared to fight again until he spotted the shape of an American helmet moving toward him. "I yelled at them: Give me some water! I was really thirsty. He looked at me and said: You're shot in the stomach. I can't give you water. So I asked him for some morphine. I told him I had used mine up on the other wounded (and) it really hurts. He said: You're shot in the head. I can't give you morphine. So I said: Well, then give me a cigarette. He gave me that."

Eade spent a year in the Army Hospital at Valley Forge. While he was there Barry Burnite's mother came to see him. "She asked me how did her son die. I kind of told her the truth and I kind of didn't. I cleaned it up a bit. The uncontrollable grief of that woman has stayed with me my whole life. Her pain and grief was more than I could bear to look at. I can never think about it without wanting to cry."

Now on this long-awaited return to Albany, Gwin, Forrest, and Smith began searching, each for his own piece of this ground. Each of them searching out the places where their own nightmares were born.

Here Gwin peered, with tears in his eyes, into the camera lens and declared: "There is no glory in war—only good men dying terrible deaths." Forrest looked at the tangle of brush and tall grass where the enemy ambush had snapped on that long column of American soldiers and thought back to the 600-yard run he had made right through the heaviest of the fighting to get back to his soldiers, his company, at the tail end of the column. His two radio operators, running behind him, were both killed. Forrest lost seventeen of his men killed at Albany and had tormented himself for many years wondering what he might have done to save them. The truth was that Forrest's company suffered the fewest casualties of any company that fought at Albany, in large part because their commander knew he had to get back to his men, and did.

It is only a couple of miles from X-Ray to Albany but we found a world of difference. The deep peace we found at X-Ray was not to be found at Albany. It was eerie and haunted by the spirits of soldiers who died in that grass and jungle, separated from each other. Here lay wounded Americans, intermingled with wounded North Vietnamese, and only the enemy moved among them in the darkness collecting theirs and killing ours. That and the American artillery shells and napalm canisters that killed friendly and enemy alike. In the tropical heat we shuddered with cold chills and heard the faint echoes of men screaming in pain and begging for mercy in their last seconds on earth.

Gwin said, "What I saw at Albany set me back. The place is evil—dank with jungle rot and an inch of water over the landing zone. I passed foxholes, still there, their square forms filled with putrescent and stagnant water. Shell holes and bomb craters were clearly visible and some of the trees were still blackened by the napalm attacks."

None of the three enemy commanders, General An, Colonel Thuoc, and Colonel Hao, had fought at Albany. An, in his bunker on the slopes of Chu Pong, thought his troops had ambushed my battalion in Albany. He had not known, until we told him, that at Albany his men fought our sister battalion, the 2nd Battalion 7th Cavalry. He had not noticed my battalion's departure from X-Ray by helicopter the day before, or our reinforcements from 2/7 Cavalry marching in overland to replace us. By the time the enemy attack began on November 17 the survivors of my battalion were back at Camp Holloway outside Pleiku, freshly shaved and showered and wearing our first issue of the new Army jungle fatigues. The American commander in Vietnam, Gen. William C. Westmoreland, climbed onto the hood of a jeep and addressed us, telling us we had won a great victory at LZ X-Ray. Even as he spoke to us the slaughter was beginning at LZ Albany and Westmoreland would not hear a word of the bad news until the next day, when he toured the 85th Evacuation Hospital at Qui Nhon and the scores of wounded told him of the desperate fighting at Albany.

That afternoon at Camp Holloway Brig. Gen. Richard Knowles, assistant division commander of the 1st Cavalry Division (Airmobile), called a news conference at Camp Holloway to address rumors of an ambush that had chewed up an American Infantry battalion in the Ia Drang the day before. Knowles told the crowd of reporters assembled in a big Army tent that there had been no ambush at LZ Albany. He called it a "meeting engagement" and said that there had been no massacre of Americans. Casualties were, he said, light to moderate. Joe Galloway, who had flown out to Albany that morning and saw Chinook cargo helicopters being stacked full of American bodies, stood on trembling legs and roared: "That's bullshit and you know it, General."

Back in Saigon General Westmoreland, furious because he had been briefed extensively on the victory at X-Ray by the Cavalry commanders, who spoke not a word of the unfolding debacle at Albany, picked up the phone and called the Field Force Vietnam (corps) commander, Lt. Gen. Stanley "Swede" Larsen, and demanded an explanation. Larsen said he would investigate and report back. Larsen flew to Pleiku and sat down with 1st Cavalry Division commander Maj. Gen. Harry W. O. Kinnard, assistant division commander Brigadier General Knowles, and the 3rd Brigade commander, Col. Tim Brown. He asked why none of them had told General Westmoreland about the battle at Albany. "Each of them told me that they had not told General Westmoreland about the battle because they did not know about it," Larsen told Joe years later in a telephone discussion. Afterward General Larsen provided Joe a signed affidavit detailing these events. "They were lying and I left and flew back to my headquarters and called Westy and told him so, and told him I was prepared to bring court-martial charges against each of them. There was a long silence on the phone and then Westy told me: No, Swede, let it slide."

With that began a years-long Army effort to cover up what had transpired in this haunted jungle clearing halfway around the world from home. The memoirs of Westmoreland and others speak glowingly of the battle at X-Ray but not a word is written of the battle they wanted to forget. Joe told me once that he dates the rot at the heart of our effort in Vietnam to that very moment when Westmoreland told Larsen to "let it slide." Valuable lessons are there to be learned from every battle, even the disasters or maybe especially the disasters. But you can't learn a thing from a battle you have tried to hide, for whatever reason. I thought about all this, and I know Joe did, as we walked this soggy ground where so many young Americans had been slain in what may have been some of the most vicious hand-to-hand fighting of the entire Vietnam War. Where wounded men held their breath and played dead as they heard the wounded man just a few feet away in the darkness beg for his life and receive a bullet in the head as an answer. In this place Charlie Company 2/7 Cavalry, Smith's outfit, began the day with 110 men and officers. The next day only 8 of those men were marked present for duty. The rest were either dead or wounded.

———

My first visit to this Albany battleground came in April 1966 when, after I succeeded Colonel Brown as commander of the 3rd Brigade, I led an operation back into X-Ray and Albany. We came here to Albany searching for the four Americans still listed as missing in action since November 17, 1965. Captain Forrest had moved on from company command in 1/5 Cavalry to a division staff job, but he came along on this operation because one of the missing men belonged to his company. That man had been marked down as wounded and evacuated but later Forrest received a letter from his mother saying she had not heard anything from her son in six weeks. Forrest turned the Army hospital system upside down but could not find a trace of his trooper. Now he again loped down that 600-yard-long trail where so many had died, right back to the end where his company had fought. There in the high elephant grass he found the bones, tattered uniform, and dog tags of his missing soldier, lying where he had fallen in the first burst of firing. We also located bones and identification of the other three missing 2/7 Cavalry soldiers. Graves registration crews collected all four for the beginning of their long-delayed journey home.

Before we left, as we waited for our helicopter to return and pick us up, our small group gathered once more in a circle and said a farewell prayer to the dead of this haunted place of battle.

We flew back to Pleiku and that evening our party gathered for a farewell dinner. Several of the Vietnamese would leave us here and return home to Hanoi the following day. The menu for all of us—except Plumley, who had brought his own large paper sack of rations from home, small tins of Vienna sausage and potted meat, boxes of Saltine crackers, and a squirt bottle of yellow mustard—was rice, soup, baguettes, and Ba Muoi Ba "33" beer.

Colonel Hao, during the hours while he and the others waited for news that we were safe, had written a poem which he read to us. It is reprinted, in translation, here. It touched our hearts. General An and I exchanged personal gifts during this dinner: I gave him my wristwatch. He took off his old green pith helmet with its single star on a red background and handed it to me. It is a cherished reminder of how two old enemies found friendship on their battlefield of long ago, and it hangs in a place of honor on the wall of my den.

Here is the poem Colonel Hao read to us that night:

> To remember the days of war
> We have come to you this afternoon
> Our old battlefield still here.
> Yet how do we find your graves
> Now hidden by 30 years of growth.
> In your youth like the leaves so green
> Your blood soaks the earth red
> For today's forest to grow.
> Words cannot describe how we miss you
> Our fingers trace the bark for clues of days past.
> We imagine you resting for a thousand peaceful autumns
> Feeling the loss of each of you.
> We come to rejoin a span of bridge
> For the happiness of those living.
> On a calm autumn afternoon in Ia Drang
> Veterans join hands.

Back to the Hell That Was Albany

After 30 years we relive that battle
Between two sides of the frontline.
Now we stand at each other's side
Remembering generals and soldiers of years past
Bring back the months and years of history
Untroubled by ancient rifts
We look together toward the future
Hoping that generations to come will remember.
Our people know love and bravery
We leave old hate for new friendships.
Together we will live in peace
So that this land will remain ever green
Forever in peace and harmony.

NINE

*Walking the Ground
at Dien Bien Phu*

On the troopship that carried my battalion to Vietnam in the summer of 1965 I brought a box of books, most of them histories of the French experience and war in Indochina, to read or reread in my search for useful information about the place we were bound for and the people we would fight. Among the books was Bernard Fall's superb *Hell in a Very Small Place*, a study of the pivotal 1954 Battle of Dien Bien Phu, where the French had bet everything they had and lost. I also devoured another fine history by Fall, a French-born American scholar, titled *Street Without Joy*, about the French war against the Viet Minh in the southern part of Vietnam. The lessons taught by Dr. Fall were all about treating the Vietnamese with respect as an enemy who was tough, tenacious, and a damned fine fighter.

Although most Americans were contemptuous of French fighting abilities and the usefulness of any lessons that might be learned from their experience and their defeat in Indochina, somehow I felt there was a relevance for the war we were about to fight in Vietnam; that what had happened at the Battle of Dien Bien Phu might shape battlefield decisions I would be called on to make in the months to come.

The French had a century and a half as the colonial occupier of Indochina and somehow had not learned those lessons. For nine long years, beginning in 1945, the Viet Minh nibbled away at the French in hit-and-run guerrilla attacks that began with small squads armed with ancient weapons and, under command of a former schoolteacher, Vo Nguyen Giap, slowly grew in size, skill, and ability. At the end, in the Dien Bien Phu Valley, over 13,000 French and colonial soldiers were pinned down and slowly destroyed by a Viet Minh army of some 50,000 troops supplied by 40,000 porters who hauled rice and ammunition and manhandled modern artillery pieces through the rugged mountain trails from the China border—capabilities the French commanders thought were simply impossible and unthinkable.

General Giap had urged Joe and me to visit Dien Bien Phu during our conversations in 1991 and 1993, telling us that he simply didn't understand why the Americans had not carefully studied the French war in Vietnam and the Battle of Dien Bien Phu, particularly since, by the end, the United States was financing more than 70 percent of the cost of the French military actions and providing much of the equipment and ammunition in that war. He told us if we Americans had studied what happened to the French surely we would never have come halfway around the world to take their place in Vietnam and pursue a long bloody war that ended just as badly for us as it had for the French.

In the years since the end of our war in Vietnam I had read a great deal about both the French war and ours and could see parallels, especially the fact that both the French and we Americans were foreign armies on Vietnamese soil fighting against a Vietnamese enemy determined to drive us out, no matter how long it took or how many lives it cost. Early in the rebellion against the French, General Giap quite accurately assessed the inevitable outcome for them, and his analysis was very much on point when applied to the Americans:

"The enemy will pass slowly from the offensive to the defensive. The blitzkrieg will transform itself into a war of long duration. Thus, the enemy will be caught in a dilemma. He has to drag out the war in order to win it and does not possess, on the other hand, the psychological and political means to fight a long, drawn-out war. . . ."

In the spring of 1954 I had just returned from commanding two companies fighting the bitter hill battles during the stalemate part of the Korean War—a time when negotiations for an end to the war were under way at Panmunjom and both sides were deeply entrenched in defensive bunkers and trenches trying to hold what they had and nibble away at what the enemy held. It was a terrible war, where the frigid Korean winter was almost as bad an enemy as the Chinese. The Chinese battered us with endless artillery barrages and sudden head-on assaults launched in darkness by wave after wave of thousands of tough enemy troops firing their fear-some and very effective burp guns, which were ideal for close-quarters combat. They came through our walls of defensive artillery and mortar fire and our heavy machine-gun fire seemingly without concern for their heavy casualties. There were no flanking movements or envelopment attempts. It was hey diddle diddle, straight up the middle with whistles and bugles blowing. It was unforgettable. I had been assigned to West Point as an Infantry tactical officer teaching and train-ing cadets at my old alma mater, and now my attention was drawn to the daily radio news reports of the Viet Minh siege of Dien Bien Phu in the remote mountains of the northern part of Vietnam.

What I was hearing that spring made my blood run cold. It was another bunker and trench war, this time in the tropics. The principal adviser and supplier of the Vietnamese Com-munist guerrillas was none other than Communist China. The artillery pieces now hammering away at the French strongpoints there were 105mm howitzers the Chinese had captured from U.S. forces in Korea. All I was hearing was so familiar, so terrible, and it brought back the nightmares of my own experiences. I was glued to the radio as, day by day, the Viet Minh dug and tunneled and drew their noose ever tighter around the besieged French and colonial troops. Once again I could hear that awful cry "Enemy in the trenches!" and know that the combat now would be hand-to-hand, man-to-man. My wife, Julie, couldn't understand my fascination with so distant a foreign battle and I couldn't explain it to her. My heart went out to those French troops because I knew exactly what they were going through. I had been there.

In the years after Dien Bien Phu and the French defeat I read each new book that came out on that war and that battle, little knowing that I was preparing myself to fight my own last-ditch battle against the same tough commanders who had been the victors at Dien Bien Phu—Gen. Chu Huy Man, who as a brigadier general commanded a division there, and Lt. Gen. Nguyen Huu An, who as a major commanded a regiment there.

This battle that ended the French war in Vietnam would resonate in important ways in the battle that began the American war in Vietnam in Landing Zone X-Ray eleven years later. The lessons I drew from my study of Dien Bien Phu and from my experiences in Korea were key to a pivotal decision I made on the first day at X-Ray. As the fighting raged that first afternoon the enemy boiled down off the mountain and launched attack after attack directly at our lines. I gave brief thought to the fact that as my companies arrived by helicopter I had fed all of them into sections of the perimeter that faced the mountain and the withering attacks of the enemy forces. My rear was wide open and undefended. If the enemy commander ordered some of his units to work their away around behind us they would have an open shot straight into the clearing and could strike my troops from the rear. It was then that I thought of Dien Bien Phu and Korea and how these Vietnamese commanders and their Chinese mentors had come straight into the French and American positions with little concern for trying the flanks or attempting to envelop those positions by attacking from all directions. This was how my opposite number had conducted the attacks in X-Ray so far, and while I kept my eyes open for any sudden change in his tactics I felt comfortable leaving our back door open until more troops arrived and we had the luxury of defending in every direction. It may seem a small thing, but given the enemy's far greater numbers and how thinly we were spread, holding that ragged semicircle facing the mountain, it was critical to our survival.

When the opportunity presented itself in October 1999 to visit Dien Bien Phu and walk that historic battleground, my response was swift and affirmative. Joe and I headed back to Vietnam on what would be our last trip there together, taking General Giap's advice to someday visit that remote valley where forty-five years earlier his peasant soldiers won a victory and a war that gave them their own country.

As we stepped off the Vietnamese civilian airliner at Dien Bien Phu on October 19, I stood and slowly turned through 360 degrees, taking in the brooding mountains that surrounded and looked down on this long, narrow valley. I marveled at the arrogance and stupidity of the French commander in Indochina, Gen. Henri Navarre, who bet everything he had on one card, and lost it all. When we landed the only threat left at Dien Bien Phu was a scattering of water buffalo, held at bay by half a dozen Vietnamese posted along the runway when one of the twice-weekly flights arrived or left.

It was near this concrete landing strip, in a dark damp bunker, that newly promoted French Brig. Gen. Christian de Castries surrendered to Viet Minh soldiers pointing rifles at him and ended an agonizing fifty-five-day siege that cost both sides thousands upon thousands of casualties. It also marked the end of French colonial rule in Indochina. What struck me hardest was how vulnerable the French troops had been from the first day, scattered over twelve defensive positions around and across the narrow three-mile-wide by eleven-mile-long north-south valley.

Navarre's original plan in November 1953 was to parachute six battalions into Dien Bien Phu—then a tiny crossroads village of no more than a dozen huts some 260 miles northwest of Hanoi—to block any Viet Minh threat against neighboring Laos and, hopefully, disrupt Giap's supply lines and the opium trade with mountain tribes that provided revenue to help finance the guerrilla war. But the stakes grew much higher with the scheduling of the Geneva Conference on Indochina for the spring of 1954. Navarre desperately wanted to give the French government—under heavy pressure at home to negotiate an end to the increasingly unpopular and costly war—a victory to strengthen their bargaining position. The Viet Minh leader Ho Chi Minh and his commander, Giap, wanted exactly the same thing.

So what began as a modest but daring thrust into the mountainous border region swiftly grew in importance to both sides. Navarre, a cavalryman, flew in thirty-two tanks, thinking the flat valley would be ideal terrain and that the tanks would be a decisive factor in defeating a lightly armed, poorly supplied enemy. He was wrong. The valley was subject to both a long monsoon season and poor drainage and the tanks spent more time bogged down and broken than they did maneuvering. By the time the Viet Minh launched their final assaults only two of Navarre's tanks were still operable.

But the key to the French defeat was neither armor nor foot soldiers, but artillery. De Castries had scores of 105mm and 155mm heavy artillery pieces and his artillery commander and second in command of the French force, one-armed Col. Charles Piroth, was supremely confident that any heavy guns the Viet Minh might drag to the tops of the mountains would be few in number and swiftly silenced by his guns and French air attacks. He was so confident, in fact, that the French colonel boasted that not a single enemy shell would ever land inside the French fortress.

What they and Navarre believed to be impossible was happening on the narrow dirt track that led from Dien Bien Phu back to the China border. An army of some 40,000 Vietnamese porters were pushing and pulling twenty-four 105mm American artillery guns along that trail—guns the Chinese had captured from us in Korea—along with more than 300 other artillery pieces, heavy mortars, Russian-made Katyusha rocket launchers, and antiaircraft guns. The porters hauled the ammunition for the big guns and, using the modified bicycles that became famous on the Ho Chi Minh Trail in another war, along with 17,000 horses they moved 20,000 tons of rice to the front to feed the soldiers.

The real surprise, when those guns signaled the attack before dusk on March 13, 1954, was not only that the Viet Minh had artillery but that it was perfectly emplaced and nearly invulnerable to counter-battery fire and air attacks—dug into the mountaintops from the reverse slopes, with only the barrels briefly appearing in small openings to fire and then be pulled back to safety inside the mountain.

When the first enemy shells exploded inside the French fortifications the artillery colonel who had boasted of their invulnerability and invincibility apologized to de Castries and the other commanders, then withdrew to his bunker, lay down on his bed, pulled the pin on a hand grenade, and blew himself up. He knew that the battle only now beginning was already lost—fifty-five days before the end came.

The enemy artillery, and the antiaircraft guns they had also installed on the mountains, closed the airfield at Dien Bien Phu. Dozens of transport planes were destroyed on the strip or shot down, some of them flown by American crews. The long, narrow road to Hanoi had long since been closed by Viet Minh ambushes. Now the 12,000 to 13,000 French and colonial soldiers could only be supplied by airdrops from planes forced by ack-ack fire to fly ever higher: first dropping supplies from 2,000 feet, then from 6,000 feet, and finally from 8,500 feet. Of the 120 tons of supplies dropped daily over the French positions, only 90 to 100 tons landed in the right place on a very good day. The rest—ammunition, medical supplies, wine and food—was used and appreciated by the enemy.

The French had by now been fighting the Viet Minh since the end of World War II, and one would think that their commanders would have a comprehensive understanding of Viet Minh tactics, firepower, tenacity, and fighting ability. The fourth-century B.C. Chinese master of strategy and tactics, Sun Tzu, wrote: "Know your enemy and know yourself and in a hundred battles you will never be in peril." The French commanders didn't know their enemy and now the brave but doomed garrison at Dien Bien Phu paid the price.

There is no glory in trench warfare. Life is lived underground like a mole, burrowing endlessly in the mud building new bunkers, repairing old ones collapsed by enemy artillery or unfriendly rain. Those condemned to this kind of warfare are the undead, but they have been buried nonetheless. I knew how those poor French-led troops had lived and died. In Korea and at Dien Bien Phu there were communications or commo trenches, six to eight feet deep. Some had duckboards in the bottoms; most did not. When it rained they were a deep muddy mess. There were offshoot trenches leading to fire steps and fighting positions on the spines and slopes of the hills. Also off the main trench were dugouts or bunkers used for command posts and ammunition storage. The surrounding terrain was a moonscape, stripped of any growth and pocked with water-filled pits and holes from thousands of shell and bomb explosions.

Then there was the smell, a foul miasma combined of the odors of latrines, sour-smelling wet clothes and dirty unwashed men, wet sandbags, churned mud, and gunpowder. Under a hot sun this unique perfume was thick enough to cut. Occasionally, in digging trench extensions or new firing positions, long-dead human remains were unearthed, adding yet another layer to the smell. When the monsoon torrents came—in July and August for us in Korea, and from March through May at Dien Bien Phu—for the soldiers buried deep in the earth life became pure Hell. In the Dien Bien Phu Valley twelve feet of rain falls each year, greatly multiplying that misery.

The Chinese we fought in Korea were masters with the shovel—hard-core, heavy-duty professional diggers. So too were General Giap's Viet Minh, who would later perfect their skills and dig massive miles-long underground complexes beneath the feet of patrolling American GIs in South Vietnam—subterranean military bases so cleverly built and hidden that they survived all attempts to find and destroy them and were still in business when the war ended a decade later.

Though I experienced them many times it is hard for me to describe what it is like to endure a saturation bombardment of heavy artillery in a small impact area. The noise, the dust or mud, the choking smoke, the screaming of the wounded, the sheer terror of it all is enough to unhinge the strongest of men. It is nothing less than a torrential downpour of fire and shrapnel. On Pork Chop Hill our trenches were deep, the dugouts and bunkers and parts of the trenches covered with heavy timbers and sandbags. Once the Chinese got into the system it was hard to find them and kill them in the dark. Only by listening for the sound of weapons or someone talking could the soldiers identify friend from foe. With the barbed-wire entanglements and mines it was not possible to get out of the trenches and maneuver against the enemy in the darkness.

Now Joe and I were here, on the spot, walking that same ground. All the old strongpoints, once gleefully named by French commanders either for their wives or their mistresses—Dominique, Isabelle, Beatrice, Gabrielle, Eliane, Huguette—are now heavily overgrown by the encroaching scrub brush and jungle. But many of the old trenches and firing positions remain. They are fenced off against the general public because of the danger of old unexploded shells and mines, but we were free to explore them.

At the time of the great battle there were only a few hundred inhabitants of the valley, but now Dien Bien Phu is a provincial capital and home to more than 100,000 people. The trenches and positions around and west of the airport have been erased and replaced by peaceful rice paddies where small boys herd the water buffalo. The city has grown up to the east and south of the airfield. The old Bailey bridge that spanned the Nam Youm River between Eliane and Huguette, the French command bunker, is gone, replaced by a similar stronger steel bridge. The rusting remains of an old Quad-50 machine-gun system stands silent guard over the bridge on the northwest side of the river. Two hulks of French M-24 tanks likewise guard the re-created French command bunker where de Castries surrendered.

In the desperate fifty-five days of fighting General Giap's force of nearly 50,000 soldiers suffered 23,000 casualties—8,000 killed and 15,000 wounded. De Castries's force suffered 2,242 killed and 6,463 wounded during the campaign, some of them replaced by reinforcements who were parachuted into the battle. A total of more than 6,500 prisoners, including thousands of wounded, were recorded by the Viet Minh and then marched off into captivity as prisoners after the fall of Dien Bien Phu, suffering a brutal experience that American POWs would likewise endure at the hands of the same Vietnamese Communists beginning a decade later. Those judged able-bodied were force-marched some 250 miles to detention camps. Hundreds died along the way of starvation and disease. A total of only 3,290 were repatriated after the Geneva Conference formally ended the war four months later. The fate of an estimated 3,000 prisoners from Dien Bien Phu is still unknown.

While we were there Joe and I drove out Provincial Route 41 and a portion of Route 19, over which Giap's porters supplied his forces, to see the general's headquarters—or what is purported to be a re-creation of his headquarters. Contemporary photographs in Fall's book about Dien Bien Phu show Giap in a headquarters near a waterfall. What we were shown was a location a three-quarter-mile hike up a concrete path, with a small stream on the left, in a heavily wooded draw. A tunnel through a finger of the draw leads from the staff area to a small, spartan re-creation in concrete of a palm frond shelter that was labeled Giap's office and sleeping area. Even today Route 19 is narrow, full of hairpin turns, the shoulders heavily eroded by the monsoons. The Viet Minh must have had a terrible time keeping it open and repaired for the army of porters hauling supplies during the buildup and siege.

On our return to town we briefly visited the Military Museum, a poorly maintained building at the end of an overgrown walkway. Outdoors there was an area of shot-up remains of French vehicles, aircraft, and artillery pieces in bad shape; the Viet Minh mortars, ack-ack guns, and artillery were pristine. The centerpiece of the museum was a huge terrain model of the battlefield and surrounding mountains half the size of a tennis court. Across the street is one of three military cemeteries where thousands of Viet Minh dead from Dien Bien Phu's battles are buried, their names inscribed on a memorial wall erected in 1994 during the fortieth anniversary observation. Nearby is the entrance to the hilltop position the French named Eliane. We briefly visited that position; then moved on to Beatrice; then Gabrielle, and finally the re-created de Castries command bunker near the airstrip. Beatrice and Gabrielle were both overrun and captured by the Viet Minh on the first two days of battle, March 13 and 14, respectively.

Our visit was hurried and I asked permission to return the

following day with the Vietnamese translator Tien and the official minder assigned to our party. We hiked up the steep path to Beatrice, where the old trenches are now only three to four feet deep, filled in by forty-five years of erosion. From there we went to Gabrielle, the northernmost and most isolated of the strongpoints. The elongated hilltop position was crisscrossed with old trenches mostly hidden by thick thorn vines and high elephant grass. We could not traverse the position and finally went around the hill to the south end, where a monument to the victors stands not far from old dugouts that once held heavy French mortars.

Our next stop was Eliane, the last major position overrun by the Viet Minh as they attacked toward the French supply dump, hospital, and de Castries's command bunker. A monument atop the hill describes its importance in the battle. On the south side a huge hole, partly filled with water, marks where the Vietnamese tunneled under French positions and packed in hundreds of pounds of explosives, which they detonated at the beginning of the final assault.

General An, then a major, commanded the regiment of the 16th Viet Minh Division, which assaulted and captured Eliane. General Man, then a brigadier general, was the division commander. Colonel Thuoc, then a sergeant, was an assistant squad leader in An's regiment. All of them had studied in a very hard school before we had our first meeting in November 1965 in the Ia Drang Valley.

Our Dien Bien Phu trip was to be capped, when we returned to Hanoi, with a promised three-hour interview with General Giap about this battle. But we found that he was in the hospital and unable to see us. Joe and I decided to use the extra three days in Hanoi calling on General An's widow and family and having dinner at the homes of General Man and Colonel Thuoc. At the An home we were warmly welcomed by Mrs. An, her two businessman sons in suits and ties, and her daughter, a medical doctor and a major in the People's Army of Vietnam. A spacious living room had been turned into a combination shrine and museum to the memory of General An, who died of a heart attack three years after our visit to the Ia Drang battlefields. I grieved for my old enemy and new friend at the time, and wrote to his family offering my sympathy for their great loss. My feeling of loss grew out of my respect for an officer and commander whose career in many ways mirrored my own. When we arrived in Hanoi I sent a message to An's family asking if I might call on them to pay my respects. On the advice of our Vietnamese translator, Joe and I brought a bouquet of white lilies and a large packet of incense.

When we arrived we were ushered into a large living and dining room. Along one wall was a Buddhist shrine with a large portrait of An before a table containing fruit, flowers, and incense holders. We added our flowers and I lit the bundle of sandalwood incense. Next to the shrine was a large glass-fronted display case containing the general's dress uniform, his medals, albums of photographs An had taken during his long career, the letter of sympathy I had written, the wrist-watch I had given him in the Ia Drang, and a copy of *We Were Soldiers Once . . . and Young* we had inscribed and signed and sent to him when it was first published. Mrs. An sat us down and proudly showed us several large photo albums depicting the impressive state funeral General An was accorded as a real hero of Vietnam's revolution and wars. Thousands of soldiers marched at An's last review. I hoped his final resting place was among soldiers and that some of his old comrades from Dien Bien Phu and the Ia Drang were nearby to keep him company.

Our dinners at the homes of General Man and Colonel Thuoc were likewise cordial and filled with discussion of their memories of the Dien Bien Phu battle. We were received warmly as old friends. General Man was by now retired from active duty and living with his daughter and her husband and several grandchildren. All traces of his previous formality were gone. He had traded his general's uniform for a natty sports coat and an open-collared shirt. I thought back to our first interview with him and how, afterward, Joe chuckled as we walked back to our quarters in the two-rat Army hotel. He said he had a vision that one day Man's engineer son would burst in shouting to the old revolutionary: "Dad, you'll never guess who is the new country manager for IBM."

A few years after that trip Joe and I were at a conference on Vietnam for nongovernmental organizations in the Washington, D.C., suburbs. A woman rushed up to Joe and asked if he had written the book about the Ia Drang. He said he had. She said: "You wrote in your book about General Chu Huy Man?" Joe again said yes. She said: "You'll never guess who we have sponsored for a scholarship to study at the Colorado School of Mines—General An's son!" That same year another Vietnamese we met on our first trip, the press counselor at the Vietnam embassy in Bangkok, was studying at Harvard on a Nieman Fellowship.

Our visit to the home of Joe's good friend Colonel Thuoc was no less interesting. On our trip to the Ia Drang, Joe and the colonel were seatmates on the bus and got acquainted. It was Thuoc who tapped Joe on the chest with one finger and said: "You have the heart of a soldier; the same heart as mine. I am glad I didn't kill you." Thuoc showed Joe the little diaries he kept and wrote in every day of his ten years of combat in the south. Now he told Joe he had had the diaries copied and was willing to give him a copy of what he wrote during his time fighting at Dien Bien Phu. Joe asked for a copy of all his journals, and later that evening Thuoc handed them over and expressed the hope that someday he would be able to visit the United States. The translating of our conversation that evening was done by Thuoc's son, whose command of English was quite good.

At the time we were fighting these men and men like them in our long-ago war there were those on our side who denied them their humanity, who spoke of our enemies as if they were robots who served an alien cause, Communism, only because some commissar had a gun pointed at the back of their heads. No thought was given to the possibility that they were fighting so hard because, like America's own revolutionaries, they had a burning desire to drive the foreigners out of their native land; that nationalism was a far more compelling reason for them to fight than Communism. They were good soldiers, implacable foes in battle, and now that the guns had fallen silent and peace had returned to their land they proved to be proud fathers, good husbands, loyal citizens, and, yes, good friends.

TEN

The Never-Ending Story

The next morning, October 20, our smaller party loaded into the vans and set off down Route 14 through coffee plantation country bound for the old mountain town of Ban Me Thuot, the first provincial capital to fall to the North Vietnamese Army campaign in the early spring of 1975 that ended with the fall of Saigon and the surrender of all South Vietnamese forces.

We stopped the convoy at the Chu Dreh Pass, where the last battalion of the French Groupe Mobile 100 was ambushed and destroyed by the Viet Minh, even as the rest of that proud regiment was slaughtered in a similar ambush in the Mang Yang Pass. It was a perfect site for an ambush—with the narrow road passing through a jungled defile. Once the

Vietnamese had knocked out the vehicles leading and trailing the column of trucks, jeeps, and lightly armored vehicles, the French were trapped like sitting ducks. This was where the French fought their last engagement of the Indochina War.

We paused in Ban Me Thuot—where Teddy Roosevelt once hunted tigers on a world tour—and all of us, minus Sergeant Major Plumley, tucked into a lunch of pho, steaming bowls of Vietnamese beef soup. Plumley sat in his front-row seat on the bus chowing down, as before, on his canned sausages and crackers. "I ain't putting anything in my mouth on this trip that didn't come over with me in this bag," the sergeant major told Joe. "I promised Mrs. Plumley that I wouldn't bring anything unhealthy home with me."

Our convoy loaded up and headed east on Highway 21—a sparsely traveled remote mountain road that in 1975 was dubbed "the Trail of Tears" as a large, panicked horde of some 200,000 Vietnamese civilian refugees and South Vietnamese soldiers attempting to flee the Central Highlands was ambushed, harassed, and chopped to pieces by Viet Cong and North Vietnamese forces before they could reach the coast in a scene that would be played out all over the country in the coming weeks. It was estimated that half of the refugees in that ill-fated column on this road died.

For us it was a long rough ride over the narrow, potholed route rising toward yet another remote mountain pass, which we reached long after dark. There we narrowly escaped an ambush. Our drivers slammed on the brakes as their headlights picked out a line of large rocks blocking the road. General An, our escorts and drivers piled out and swiftly cleared the rocks away. A hundred yards past the roadblock we caught up with two barefooted men, AK-47 rifles slung over their backs, pedaling their bicycles furiously down the hill. Since none of our Vietnamese were armed they were left unchallenged to pedal down the mountain toward home.

Had there been only one van, not four, and no uniformed Vietnamese military men, there's little doubt in my mind that we would have been relieved of our money and valuables by those barefoot highwaymen, whose hard labor building the roadblock was fruitless this time.

We spent that night at a comfortable old hotel on the beach at Nha Trang and enjoyed a late dinner of langouste, a delicious South China Sea relative of the lobster. Another party of 1st Cavalry veterans, traveling separately from us, had already taught the hotel pianist the old 7th Cavalry regimental marching tune "Garry Owen," and he hammered out that lilting Irish drinking song vigorously, if not well.

The next morning we said our farewells to General An and to colonels Hao and Thuoc, who had arrived in Nha Trang via a different route. They were heading for the airport to catch a flight home to Hanoi. In the case of General An it was a farewell more final than any of us knew. My old enemy and new friend died just three years afterward of heart problems. He didn't live long enough to follow through on our mutually agreed plan to build a small monument in Landing Zone X-Ray in memory of all the brave soldiers, Vietnamese and American, who had perished there.

Our much-reduced traveling squad now headed south down Highway 1 toward Ho Chi Minh City, formerly Saigon, a grueling twelve-hour run. We passed by the huge port facility at Cam Ranh Bay, built by the Americans during the war, and paused for lunch at a seaside café in Phan Thiet. As we drew nearer to the city we passed through Xuan Loc, where the South Vietnamese 18th Division held off the North Vietnamese for ten days in the closing days of the war. It was at Xuan Loc that the South Vietnamese air force dropped a large American-supplied fuel-air bomb on advancing North Vietnamese troops, killing many of them in a particularly hideous fashion. At ground level, the fuel-air bomb releases a cloud of an explosive gas like propane. After a brief delay to allow the gas to settle into bunkers and foxholes a spark ignites the cloud. Those within the invisible gas cloud die a terrible death from the concussion, fire, and lack of oxygen. The North Vietnamese commanders sent a message to the South Vietnamese threatening to put Saigon to the sword if the fuel-air weapon was used again. That ended that.

Once we reached Bien Hoa, a major American air base during the war, we began to get a feel for what had happened to Saigon in the intervening years. Bien Hoa once was a separate town twenty miles outside Saigon with rice paddies and farm fields in between. Now we found that Saigon had grown out to meet Bien Hoa as millions more rural Vietnamese migrated to the big city for economic reasons. The farmland was now filled with shantytowns of small, crudely built shacks with few amenities that housed that population boom.

We saw the new Vietnam that has emerged from the ashes of war. The Saigon we knew had grown topsy-turvy, and as we reached the heart of the old city the streets were jammed with motorbikes, bicycles, cars, trucks, buses, and pedestrians. In this year of our visit, 1993, we bunked down at the old and then unrestored Caravelle Hotel, once headquarters of legions of American war correspondents like Dan Rather and Tom Brokaw and visitors to the war like Walter Cronkite. Across the way, past the old French Opera House, the fabled Continental Hotel had already been refurbished and its "Continental Shelf"—the famous open-air terrace restaurant where journalists from Graham Greene to Hunter Thompson once mingled over cold *citron pressés* with soldiers, diplomats, spies, and adventurers in the afternoon heat—was now glassed in, air-conditioned, and sadly more civilized and less rowdy. Soon other notable downtown Saigon hotels, such as the riverfront Majestic, the Brinks and Rex Officer Quarters, and the Caravelle itself, would be spiffed up and reborn as four- and five-star hotels where a good room costs $300 a night and up.

Another sign of great change: Joe and I went to dinner the next night at the home of the sister of a Vietnamese friend of Joe's who was a photographer for UPI during the war and now lives in California. She and her husband lived in a huge modern villa, with an Olympic-size swimming pool, in a section of the city known as Beverly Hills. She and her husband are the Vietnam representatives of one of the major Japanese electronics manufacturers. They live like millionaires, and are, their business and many others flourishing as Vietnam's ruling Communist Party welcomed foreign investments and opened doors to trade and commerce.

Vietnam today—in late 2007, as this is written—is skillfully and delicately balanced between neighboring giant China and its old enemy/new friend the United States; between Communism and capitalism; between a rock and a hard place. Two-way trade with the United States was nearly $9 billion in 2006; over $9 billion with China that same year. There is an American embassy in Hanoi; an American consulate in Ho Chi Minh City. The nation is ruled by the Communist Party politburo and Central Committee, and while it has lifted its foot off the throat of the economy and unleashed the business-man hidden in the heart of every Vietnamese, the hard-liners still brook no word of dissent or protest. The Montagnard and Hmong tribes of the Central Highlands, especially those who have embraced Christianity, have fared badly since the war's end. U.S. diplomats have pressed the government on the issue of human rights, as did George W. Bush when he became the first American president to visit Vietnam, without notable success.

Both Hanoi and old Saigon have experienced bursts of growth that are phenomenal to those who have visited Vietnam periodically during the years since the American war ended in 1975. High-rise office towers and hotels dot the skylines and the construction of more of both continues unabated. In Hanoi the authorities must patrol the vital dikes that protect the city from the Red River floods, tearing down the houses and shops of squatters who daily encroach on them. There are housing developments for the newly wealthy where building lots go for half a million dollars. In this hothouse economy corruption is endemic. The Ho Chi Minh City of today is crowded beyond belief and navigating across the main bou-levards against a phalanx of motor scooters and motorbikes forty or fifty abreast is nothing short of a dance of death. Locals advise visitors on the rules and etiquette of surviving a street crossing as a pedestrian: One must step confidently off the curb and move just as confidently into the stream of traffic, moving at a steady pace without looking at the motorcyclists or making any sudden stop or speedup. The motorcyclists will adjust for you as long as they can count on that. Otherwise you will be hit and a huge pile of motorbikes will land on you when you go down.

The girlie bars of Tu Do, where young women clad in *ao dai*, the graceful and sensuous native dress, hustled GIs for watered-down drinks are long gone. In their place are shops hustling the latest in Japanese electronics, jewelry, and souvenirs for the tourists. But the more things change, the more they remain the same: Young men furtively press brochures on passing visitors that advertise special massages up the stairways that flank the shops. Near the hotels are small stalls whose owners hawk newly produced GI dog tags and knockoff Zippo lighters engraved with the insignia of American combat units and the slogan of a long-ago war to passing tourists: "When I die I'll go to Heaven, cause I've served my time in Hell."

Vietnam is hooked up to the Internet and more than 20 million Vietnamese have their homes and offices wired in to the rest of the world. Hotels even in distant provincial capitals like Hue and Danang offer your choice of wired or wireless broadband at no extra charge. Cable and satellite television are everywhere.

Joe was in Vietnam in April 2005, when he traveled from Hanoi to Hue to Quang Tri to the Ben Hai River, marking the old border between north and south, then to Ho Chi Minh City for the thirtieth anniversary of the fall of South Vietnam, a strangely muted celebration. The victory parade began at 7:00 a.m. and the public was barred from attending.

Police stood guard three blocks on either side of the parade route, turning away all but officially approved spectators and the media. The government sent Gen. Vo Nguyen Giap, then ninety-three years of age, to be the top man on the reviewing platform. The old revolutionary stood there and witnessed a parade that included floats advertising American Express and Visa, with pretty Vietnamese girls dancing around waving huge credit cards over their heads. What must the old revolutionary have been thinking of the way things turned out? Had the Communists won the war only to lose the peace?

Because of our many trips, between 1990 and 2005, we have seen the transformation of both Hanoi and the former Saigon: Hanoi, seen first in 1991, was a dingy backwater outpost bent under decades of strict wartime Communist rule, with only one private restaurant, the scars of war plainly evident and the buildings seemingly unpainted since the French left in 1954. From that bleak picture, the Vietnamese capital in just over a decade morphed into a bustling metropolis with hundreds of new restaurants and clubs, from no life to a vibrant nightlife. Cranes tower over construction sites where skyscraper office towers and new hotels are rising.

The other, Ho Chi Minh City, always had a hustler's heart and soul, and it bowed before its stern new masters from the north with all the mock subservience it showed others who came as occupiers and left, defeated, with empty pockets. Old Saigon taught the newest masters how business is done. The old Saigon is New York to Hanoi's Washington, D.C.— bigger, busier, throbbing with life, and always ready to make a deal. The new city is better, too. That which is old is made new: open sewers and fetid canals are now covered, garbage is collected, and streets are swept. The familiar stench of those sewers and canals has been traded for the smog of a million motorbikes and fleets of Mercedes-Benzes and Toyotas.

For our party of American veterans and the ABC crews the journey was near an end. We flew to Bangkok, spent a night there, and boarded a plane for home, each with his own memories, old and new, of Vietnam the war and Vietnam the country. We had, all of us, been brought up short by old painful memories of combat in the Vietnam that was, and startled by the realities of what had happened to the country and the people since we left them. If we had come here seeking closure, seeking to consign those memories to some hidden dustbin of history, we had failed. Some things are not meant to be forgotten or easily tucked away. The vision of infantry combat, the sight of young men killing and dying at close quarters, is surely one of those things. Look at the old soldiers in Ken Burns's 2007 World War II documentary *The War* and see them weep as they talk of what they saw and did in a war that ended more than six decades ago. There is no such thing as closure for soldiers who have survived a war. They have an obligation, a sacred duty, to remember those who fell in battle beside them all their days and to bear witness to the insanity that is war.

But we did find a measure of peace on our battlefields, a sense that the passage of years had at least allowed nature to heal war's scars to the red earth of the Ia Drang. We could take heart, as Jack Smith did, in seeing that flowers now bloom in soil fertilized by the blood of thousands of men. We could press one of those flowers between the pages of memory to surprise and soothe us as we flip through those pages in the quiet hours of night.

ELEVEN

Lessons on Leadership

Show me the leader and I will know his men.
Show me his men and I will know their leader.

—ARTHUR W. NEWCOMB

I am in the winter of my life now and have spent much of that life leading people, reading people, leading myself, being led, and studying leaders and leadership. I want to share with you what I've learned—the Dos and Don'ts—the principles and maxims that have shaped my life, and offer some examples of how I have applied these lessons during that life.

The date was February 12, 1940. I was on the last day of being seventeen, sick in bed recovering from pneumonia. Earlier I had decided that I wanted to try for an appointment to the U.S. Military Academy at West Point in hope of becoming an infantry officer. In pursuit of that goal I had written my congressman and the two U.S. senators from Kentucky seeking that West Point appointment without success for two years. I had not given up hope.

Late that dark, cold February afternoon my dad came home and immediately came to the bedroom where my mother was tending me. He wasted no time. The local representative of U.S. Senator A. B. "Happy" Chandler had informed Dad that the senator had a patronage job opening in the Senate Book Warehouse in Washington—and it was mine if I wanted it. The pay was $30 a week. He needed an answer immediately, and if the answer was "yes" I would leave early the next morning. Dad said he would accompany me and help me find a room in D.C. and find a doctor to care for me.

Dad said the principal of my local prep school had agreed to allow me to graduate with my class in June if I could accrue the necessary credits in English and algebra from a Washington school.

Immediately and instinctively I knew that this offer was very likely the only real chance I had to obtain an appointment to West Point—there in Washington, where such plums are handed out, as opposed to begging letters mailed from the backwoods of Kentucky.

This was my first real challenge where I had to make an immediate, time-critical decision based largely on what my instincts told me. I said yes. My mother broke into tears and we packed a suitcase. My dad and I left Bardstown at five a.m. the next day, February 13, my eighteenth birthday. We spent the night in West Virginia and reached Washington, D.C., on February 14 in the afternoon.

We found a room for me in the home of an elderly couple,

got me registered in night school, and visited a doctor for treatment of my pneumonia. Then I reported for work in the Senate Warehouse. My life had changed direction suddenly and drastically.

Later I realized I had *trusted my instincts* when I decided to accept that Washington opportunity. During the next three months I finished high school at night, studying alongside cab-drivers and government workers, got the credits transferred back to Kentucky for graduation, and registered for night school at George Washington University, which I attended for two years, year-round.

Every month I pored over the list from the War Department of unfilled West Point appointments and went knocking on the doors of senators and congressmen on Capitol Hill trying to persuade one of them to give me that appointment. I had no luck in the beginning, but I kept studying that list and walking the halls of Congress.

In short, *I NEVER QUIT*—a firm principle of self-leadership in any endeavor.

Nearly two years later, on December 7, 1941, Pearl Harbor was attacked and the world changed overnight. America went to war. Six months later President Franklin D. Roosevelt signed legislation granting every senator and representative an additional appointment to both the Military and Naval academies. The wartime Army and Navy desperately needed commissioned officers as we began urgently expanding the military from fewer than half a million troops to 15 million.

I immediately went to Senator Chandler's office and was told that he was appointing another young man to West Point. Next I visited my congressman's office (Rep. Ed Creal, 4th

District of Kentucky), and he told me that he had given his West Point slot to another boy. But the congressman told me that he would give me his appointment to the Naval Academy. I was surprised, as I had not asked for it. I thanked him and then a novel, instinctive thought hit me and I asked him: What if I can find another congressman who would appoint me to West Point in exchange for Representative Creal's Naval Academy appointment?

Representative Creal was startled and surprised, but after a moment's thought he agreed to that if I could pull it off. It took me less than a week to obtain my West Point appointment from Congressman Eugene E. Cox of the 2nd District of Georgia, in exchange for the Naval Academy slot I had in my pocket.

These events, truly a life-changing episode, and other such major turning points in my life in the years to come were the result of key decisions I made based on a number of principles, guidelines, and rules of behavior I was developing and thinking through for myself. Let's take a look at them.

First, over two years earlier when my father told me about that Washington job offer, I *instinctively* knew that was my best chance of getting into West Point. I trusted my instincts then and have done so ever since.

Trust your instincts. They are sometimes called a hunch, a gut feeling, intuition, or a sixth sense, and they are part of every person's makeup. They are the product of your personality, education, experience, reading, training, observations, and the environments in which one has lived and worked.

When seconds count and time is critical, instincts come into play in judgment and decision making. Instinct can provide a caution light; a heightened focus; an early-warning system. It is a distillation of what you know and who you are, and on occasion can lead you to a far better decision than one based on a logical process that considers all the pros and cons. In a quickly developing situation when a leader must act fast, the decision is largely based on instincts. Hunches are often more accurate or predictive than the analytical reasoning—a time-consuming exercise you no longer have time to conduct when seconds count.

When time permits, I use both intuition and analysis. I get all the information, look into the pros and cons of the options, then back off for a few hours or overnight using one or both of two approaches. One is to reach a tentative decision at day's end but not announce it. Instead I sleep on it and see how it feels the next morning when my mind is fresh. The other approach I have found valuable is to go to the gym for a good hard workout. I am not medically qualified to explain how and why, but new ideas and thoughts and often a better decision come to me when I exercise and break a sweat.

A helpful rule of thumb that I learned at West Point from a trusted mentor is *"If there's a doubt in your mind, there's no doubt at all."* In other words, if you have any reservations at all then the answer is "no." But if my head tells me one thing and my gut another—I will usually go with my gut, listen to my instincts.

When Representative Creal offered me that appointment to the Naval Academy, I immediately thought about that possible swap. I didn't know if the congressman would be willing, or even whether such an idea could be carried out under the rules on the Hill. It took only seconds for me to exercise what would become another useful lesson during my life. In situations like this, *Never say no to yourself. Make the other guy say no.*

The successful outcome of my search for a West Point appointment also illustrates another principle I have found useful: *There's always one more thing you can do to influence any situation in your favor—and after that one more thing, and after that. . . .* The more you do the more opportunities arise.

At age twenty, having just arrived three months before at West Point, I learned two great lessons that I have applied throughout my life. I had worked hard for over two years to get there—working days, going to school nights, and walking the halls of Congress in search of my dream. Finally, I made it and reported to West Point on July 15, 1942.

By the end of October my name was on the list of cadets severely deficient in grades in solid geometry and advanced algebra. I was in grave danger of flunking out, being dismissed from the Academy in December, seeing my dream go down in flames unless I brought those grades up. I was shocked and frightened that I might lose everything I had worked so hard to obtain.

From that point on, for three tough academic years, I was glued to my advanced math textbooks every night from 7:30 p.m. till lights out at 11:00 p.m.—and after lights out I moved to the nearby restroom down the hall from my room, where I sat on a toilet under a 40-watt lightbulb and continued studying until 1:00 or 2:00 a.m. If I didn't understand the advanced, arcane math and bewildering engineering, physics, and chemistry, I could at least memorize the procedures.

I made it through the academic trials and tribulations and graduated in 1945 very near the top of the bottom 20 percent of my class. I may not have mastered mathematics at West Point but I learned how valuable those two lessons are in life: *Never quit!* And: *There's always one more thing you can do to influence any situation in your favor!*

Another example that illustrates that principle came as I prepared for my entry into West Point. I was reading the Army booklet on West Point appointments and requirements for admission and learned that the Army would give an aspirant a preliminary physical exam that could reveal any problem that might bar admission. I took such a preliminary physical at Walter Reed Hospital and learned that I was "red-green color-blind" in the fainter shades of those colors and that I also needed some dental work done.

I had my teeth fixed and got a copy of the Army's color perception test book and memorized it. When I took my final physical at Fort Knox for admission, they didn't use the test I had memorized; they asked me to identify the colors of various pieces of yarn, and that I passed without a problem.

I also found out that an applicant could be admitted without taking the written examination if his high school and college grades were high enough and comprehensive enough to eliminate the need of a written exam. I submitted my grades and was excused from taking the written exam. *One more thing!!* Stack the deck!!

A leader must find or make the time to detach himself from an ongoing critical situation or daily life and ask and answer these two questions:

- What am I not doing that I should be doing to influence the situation in my favor?
- What am I doing that I should not be doing?

By asking and answering those questions frequently in a crisis you begin to shape the battlefield or the playing field in your favor; you begin to get ahead of the curve.

A senior executive is paid to do three things:

- Get the job done and get it done well.
- Plan ahead. Be proactive and not reactive. Create the future.
- Exercise good, sound judgment in the doing of it all.

To get the job done, you must have a clearly defined goal or goals and a clear understanding of what it takes to achieve those goals. You will do well to give thought to a wide variety of factors that may have an impact on your chosen course for good or ill. A good leader will continually tell and retell his people what those goals are and what their roles are in attaining those goals.

Leaders must have a workable plan, and a system of measuring progress. Subordinate leaders must understand the goal, the plan, and their role in its execution. A very important part in planning is to think through the positive and negative what-ifs before they occur and how they should be handled if they arise—especially the negative ones.

In the Korean and Vietnam combat zones while creating a plan for an operation, and after it kicked off, I always thought through the what-ifs and had my operations and intelligence officers do the same. What if this happens? What if the enemy does that? What if this subordinate leader is wounded or killed? The best leader in any enterprise anticipates problems and has plans if problems arise. He also has thought through ways to take advantage of positive openings that often occur in fleeting windows of time.

A critical part of success for any work unit is teamwork and motivation. There's a mentally reinforcing connection between discipline and confidence that results in motivated, smooth-running teamwork. By discipline I do not mean punishment or admonitions.

There are four key points for harnessing discipline in any endeavor:

1. Self-discipline leads to self-confidence.
2. Disciplined use of technology creates confidence in those tools.
3. Disciplined leaders create and foster confidence and trust in themselves by their subordinates.
4. Team discipline leads to team confidence.

A team with leaders and followers at all levels who strive to achieve these four levels of discipline will be motivated, efficient, and successful.

The second responsibility of a leader, *creating the future*, requires that you be proactive, not reactive. Acuity, insight, seeing the trends, analyzing them correctly, having a vision, and having confidence in that vision are all vital to creating the future. A good leader will inspire and motivate himself and his people to shape and create a positive future even as he deals with today and today's challenges. Check up to make certain today's jobs are getting done even as you stack the deck for future success. Keep up the momentum.

Senior leaders who push the power and the decision-making authority down free up talent in their subordinates even as they free up more of their own time to plan ahead. I am convinced that micromanager workaholic leaders who are heavily involved in the minutiae of day-to-day actions run the risk of neglecting the future of their enterprise.

The author and thinker Peter Drucker hit the nail on the head: "Even the mightiest company will be in trouble if it does not work toward the future. It will lose distinction and leader-ship. All that will be left is big company overhead. By daring not to take the risk of making the new happen, management takes by default the greater risk of being surprised by what will happen."

There are a number of other principles—some mine, some drawn from men I admire, like Gen. Colin Powell—that will help anyone be a better, more effective leader:

- Be dead honest and totally candid with those above and below you.
- There must be total loyalty, up *and* down the chain of command.
- If you have to take a subordinate to the woodshed do it in private. Praise someone in public; correct or counsel him privately. Never

take a subordinate's pride and self-respect away.

- Treat everyone fair and square, without favorites. If you discover subordinates with extraordinary talent give them the toughest jobs, not the easiest ones, and mentor them.

- Stay away from higher headquarters or corporate headquarters unless summoned. No good can come of wandering aimlessly around corridors filled with bosses alert for any sign someone is underemployed.

- As you push power and decision-making authority down you must also push subsequent praise and recognition for outstanding unit performance down as well. Don't hog the glory for yourself if you want to build a superb team.

- Good leaders don't wait for official permission to try out a new idea. In any organization if you go looking for permission you will inevitably find the one person who thinks his job is to say "No!" It's easier to get forgiveness than permission.

- The leader in the field is always right and the rear echelon wrong, unless proved otherwise. Shift power and accountability to the people who are bringing in the beans, not the ones who are counting or analyzing them.

Bookstores are filled with tomes on leadership and management. You can be Attila the Hun, Lee Iacocca, Jack Welch—or a 3-minute manager. All promise to reveal the "secrets" of effective leadership. But there are no secrets; only common sense. I have dozens of well-thumbed books on leadership in my library. I have spent a lifetime involved with leadership—good and bad. Being led, leading myself and others, reading about leaders, learning from my mistakes, successes, and experience of others.

But of all the tips, tenets, and principles I talk about here and list above, the ones about people are the ingredients that make any leadership recipe work. People are the most important part of any organization. This is why leadership is an art; management is a science. Leadership is about getting people to do what you want them to do, and that requires all we've said here and more. Above all it demands that you care deeply about those you are leading. You must care about their training, the quality of their lives, about their todays and their tomorrows. Without this love of the people who stand with you in pursuit of success, leadership is doomed to failure sooner or later. As I told the cadets at my farewell lecture at West Point in the spring of 2005, of all the principles and tenets and rules of leadership the greatest of them all is *love*.

Love is not a word military leaders throw around easily but it is the truth as I know it. Especially if you are a military leader. You must love what you are doing, because the rewards are few and the risks and hardships many. You must love the soldiers who serve under you, for you will ask everything of them, up to and including their precious lives. You must put their care and comfort ahead of your own in all matters large and small. As a leader you don't eat until they have eaten; you don't see to your own needs until you have met all theirs. Loyalty must flow downward first, then it will be returned tenfold when it is needed. I realize there are differences in military and civilian leadership, but in my opinion these bedrock principles based on love are universal.

My experience during military service and afterward in business has shown me that there are at least two categories of what ifs in any endeavor: those that you can do something about, and those you cannot. Either way it is a grave mistake not to plan for them. Be ready.

I never was comfortable with taking on a lot of risk that was out of my control or could have disastrous consequences if a situation went sour. On the battlefield when taking a bold risk, my staff and I carefully calculated it with detailed forethought not only to make it work, but to think through contingency plans on what we would do if we ran into trouble from any direction. It is very important to have a plan to follow through so you can exploit success when you are blessed with it.

A common theme running through books and stories about great leaders is while they made sure they knew what the pitfalls and negatives were, rather than fretting and worrying about them, they dwelled instead on how to avoid or defeat them. As Sun Tzu, the great Chinese scholar, wrote in the fourth century B.C., "Know your enemy and know yourself: and in a hundred battles you will never be in peril." On the business battlefields that principle could be paraphrased: "Know your competition, know your capabilities, know your market, and know yourself and you will succeed."

Despite detailed preparation, when events do not go as

planned, when you are sideswiped by adversity, face up to the facts and deal with them. No whining; no "if onlys." You can't change the facts—but there's always one more thing you can do to influence any situation in your favor. There's always a way!

On the first afternoon in the LZ X-Ray battle, when I had only 200 or so of my men on the ground, we were strongly attacked by around 1,200 enemy. They were determined to kill us all. I called in maximum air and artillery fire and was determined that we would prevail. I briefly thought about how the back side of our perimeter was wide open, but that was not my major concern. We were being hit by a fierce frontal attack—just as that same enemy army had struck the French positions at Dien Bien Phu. Remembering this from studies of that French battle, I paid little attention to my wide-open rear and it was the right decision.

You can read those leadership and management books till the cows come home or Hell freezes over, but if you want it boiled down, good leadership revolves around *judgment*. That is the defining characteristic of a good leader. Some think that character is the key to leadership, with its implication of strict adherence to a stern code of ethics, integrity, honesty, personal morals, mental strength, and toughness. I disagree. If a leader has good judgment he or she already has the character and integrity to choose the harder right over the easier wrong. Yet you can have character and integrity and still exercise bad judgment. How?

Any of these ills—incomplete or wrong information, stress, a tired mind, a weary body, poor advice, ignoring good advice, personal ego or pride, or a poor analysis of the situation—can push a leader of character and integrity over the

Capt. Hal Moore on T-Bone Hill during the Korean War.

First Cavalry Division soldiers exercising on board the USMS *Maurice Rose* en route to Vietnam.

Lt. Col. Hal Moore, commander 1/7 Cavalry, Vietnam, 1965.

Moore and his right-hand man, Capt. Greg "Matt" Dillon,
and Lt. Col. John Burney, 1966.

Hal Moore and Joe Galloway at the Vietnam Veterans Memorial in Washington, D.C.

View from the back of our hotel in Dien Bien Phu. This one was without rats!

Moore and Gen. Vo Nguyen Giap in Hanoi.

Moore and Gen. Chu Huy Man, senior North Vietnamese commander in the Ia Drang battles.

Moore and Maj. Gen. Hoang Phuong, the historian who wrote the Ia Drang after-action report.

Moore with Gen. Nguyen Huu An on the return visit to LZ X-Ray.
At end of trip, An gave his helmet to Moore.

Approaching LZ X-Ray on the return visit.

Chartered Hind helicopter landing at LZ X-Ray on the return visit.

Moore and Sgt. Maj. Basil Plumley at X-Ray during the return trip.

General Moore and General An, with Sergeant Major Plumley in the foreground, at LZ X-Ray. Colonel Hao shielded the ailing An from the sun with this umbrella.

Moore and Galloway take a break in the shade on the memorable day in LZ X-Ray. The headbands kept the sweat out of their eyes.

Muddy streets of Pleiku.

In the Vietnamese provinces, bicycles are still an important mode of transportation.

At the end of the visit to LZ X-Ray, the traveling party gathers for a group photo.

Moore boards a chopper leaving LZ X-Ray at end of the memorable visit.

Larry Gwin and George Forrest at their old battleground at LZ Albany.

Rick Rescorla at LZ Albany in 1997, on a different return visit to Ia Drang.

Tony Nadal with Major Hao and another Vietnamese "minder" at LZ Albany.

Jack Smith at LZ Albany—where he picked and pressed wildflowers as peaceful souvenirs.

Bill Beck picked up these mementos of the terrible battle at LZ X-Ray.

North Vietnamese war cemeteries, like this one at Dien Bien Phu,
dot the countryside. It is believed that such a cemetery exists near X-Ray,
but Americans have been kept away from it.

French command bunker entrance
at Dien Bien Phu.

A veteran of the Viet Minh victory
over the French at Dien Bien Phu.

An early Army photo of Rick Rescorla.

Rescorla as a colonel in
the U.S. Army Reserves.

Rescorla orders the evacuation of Morgan Stanley employees
from the World Trade Center on 9/11.

Moore and his beloved
wife, Julie.

Hal and
Julie Moore.

Theresa Null Galloway in Bali in 1971; for fifteen years, she accompanied Joe on assignments around the world.

Moore and Galloway on a condolence visit to Mrs. Nguyen Huu An's Hanoi home, where she has created a shrine to her late husband.

Moore, Galloway, and Maj. Ed "Too Tall to Fly" Freeman
lead a veterans' march at the Wall.

line into bad judgment.

Most historians agree that Gen. Robert. E. Lee was a leader of the highest character and integrity. But his poor judgment in ordering Pickett's division to charge across a half mile of open fields into the entrenched guns of the Union Army resulted in a terrible slaughter of his soldiers and General Lee's defeat at Gettysburg. The general, after the disaster, offered his resignation. That exhibited his character and integrity but did not excuse his bad judgment.

I have always been keenly interested in why leaders fail. I learned early in my career to have a trusted confidant with broad experience, sagacity, and wisdom close at hand. As I moved up I tried always to find such a person and put him directly under me as my operations officer, chief of staff, or special assistant. I wanted someone who was loyal enough to me and the unit to be the "skunk at the picnic"—to tell me candidly when he thought I was about to go off on a wrong tangent. Sometimes I agreed; sometimes not. But that was the essence of loyalty—to me, to the unit, and to the mission. General Lee had such a loyal adviser—Gen. James Longstreet—who strongly advised against sending Pickett's division on that suicidal charge, but Lee rejected that advice. When I was a battalion and brigade commander in Vietnam, my loyal adviser, my sounding board, was my S-3, or operations officer, Capt. Greg "Matt" Dillon. It was the voices of Dillon and Sergeant Major Plumley that I listened to as we prepared and planned the assault into LZ X-Ray. Once we were engaged in decisive battle there was little time for further discussion; only the hard lonely duty of command.

Another maxim I have used in my life is *When there's*

nothing going wrong, there's nothing wrong—except that nothing's wrong! This is when a leader has to be most alert and proactive.

In a work unit, in a family, or in the military, complacency and inattention can often permit an explosion of trouble. In the military the two worst examples of this were the Japanese surprise attack on Pearl Harbor and our Pacific Fleet on December 7, 1941, and the December 16, 1944, German attack in the Ardennes Forest—the Battle of the Bulge.

For me this maxim is underlined in my memory by the events at Landing Zone X-Ray in the early morning on November 15, 1965. After the previous day's hard fighting it had been a fairly quiet night, and it was still quiet in the predawn. But I was uneasy. It was too quiet. The birds were not singing. I was nagged by a gut sense that something was wrong. Nothing seemed wrong, but . . .

I immediately ordered my four companies on the defensive perimeter to send out patrols to their front—recon patrols to check for any sign of the enemy. The recon patrols forward of the Company A, B, and D defensive positions made no contact, but the patrols from Charlie Company ran straight into a large force of enemy moving forward in an assault aimed directly at the C Company defensive positions. A heavy firefight ensued as the C Company patrol, taking casualties, fought a delaying action as they fell back to friendly lines. I called in heavy air and artillery fire. That terrible battle went on for three hours, and spilled over somewhat to the adjoining companies on either flank of Charlie Company. Charlie Company suffered heavy casualties, losing all its officers killed or wounded and most of its sergeants. But the surviving troops held their ground. Had not those early-morning patrols been sent out, on a hunch, and made early contact with the enemy, the outcome could have been far more disastrous.

This early-morning battle and how it began are good examples of the idea that when things seem just fine and dandy is precisely when your instincts should begin clanging out the warning.

In a fast-moving situation instincts and intuition amount to an instant estimate of the situation. When seconds count the leader must act quickly, make the decision, impart confidence to all around him, and not second-guess his own decisions.

Let's take it from the beginning: When you are put in a position of leadership the first thing you must do is visit the people on your team. Let them see you. Briefly state your vision and outlook and let them know your primary policies, expectations, and goals. Do a lot of listening. See what's going on. Sniff the air. This is vital. The absolute worst first thing a new leader can do is go into his new office, sit at his desk, and begin shuffling papers.

In mid-July 1969, I was a one-star brigadier general and chief of plans and operations for the U.S. 8th Army in Korea. My office and my staff were in the 8th Army Headquarters in Seoul, South Korea. As part of my job I visited with military units on the front line of the Demilitarized Zone to check on the defense plans and to get to know the terrain, roads, and the principal commanders and to check that my boss's, Gen. John H. Michaelis's, orders were being carried out on the ground. I was in my office by 5:45 a.m. six days a week— and for a few hours on Sunday mornings until it was time to take my family to church.

All the military police and operations logs from across Korea from the previous night were on my desk every morning. During the later Vietnam War years of 1969–1971 Korea was a hotbed of racial tensions and heavy drug use in American military units in our Army. Altercations between black and white soldiers were frequent. Marijuana grew in the ditches and prescription drugs of every sort were readily available and cheap. Bars and houses of prostitution were thick outside the gates of all military bases and did a booming business. Many draftee soldiers kept their own woman in money, food, and lodging in the nearest Korean village.

It was just after 8:00 a.m. on a beautiful spring morning in early May 1970 when it happened. I'd been waiting for the call for a couple of hours because in the wee hours just after midnight I was awakened by my duty officer reporting that black soldiers were rioting in the two main camps of the 7th Infantry Division north of Seoul. Several buildings were burning, including the Post Library. Barracks had been trashed in fighting between soldiers. I phoned that information immediately to the chief of staff in his quarters and raced to my office.

Not long after that my intercom squawked: General Michaelis wants to see you immediately. I ran up the stairs and reported to him. "Moore, you know what's happened in the Seventh Division. It's in a hell of a shape. I've relieved the division commander. I'm going to frock you with your second star and give you command. Get up there and straighten out that screwed-up outfit!" I left immediately and headed north to the 7th Division Headquarters.

The 7th Division consisted of 16,000 officers and men. No families. No women or children. A brigade of three battalions (1,800 to 2,000 men) was on the defensive line on the DMZ dividing North and South Korea. The division was scattered over South Korea in twenty-three camps. Its headquarters was at Camp Casey, twenty-six miles north of Seoul, just outside the notorious large village of Tongduchon, with its whorehouses, bars, and drug dealers.

Given the choice of taking command of a red-hot, top-drawer, really good outfit *or* an outfit in bad shape, I'll take the one in bad shape every time, because there's no way it can go except up with strong leadership. It's always challenging and satisfying to shape up an organization in trouble. In the military and civilian organizations I've led, my principal goal was to create an institutional culture of skillful, smooth teamwork and an institutional personality of a winning outfit. A positive, upbeat institutional persona is critical in achieving success.

In any large organization, some subunits will be in excellent shape, others much less so. Some will have good leaders, some won't. Some will have people in the ranks who are troublemakers, or inefficient, or are a negative influence on the workplace environment. Some have workers who should be rewarded with recognition, promotion, more authority, and more responsibility but haven't been because of poor leadership.

All of that was true about the 7th Infantry Division when I inherited it. There was the added challenge that some of the troops were rioting and setting fires on their posts. Word of that trouble had spread swiftly throughout the 7th Division camps and stations across Korea. The officers, sergeants, and troops in the ranks were rightfully curious about their new commander and how I would tackle the situation.

When an organization is beset with problems in some areas or departments and a new boss is brought in to shape it up, he should not assume that the entire organization is rotten. He must take action quickly to stem the infection and halt its spread. In doing so he must be careful not to give the better parts of the organization the erroneous impression that the new boss is down on them, too. He should determine swiftly and accurately which subunits are in trouble and which are not before taking action. This also requires a hard look at the leadership in those units.

The first thing the new boss has to do is travel to and stand up in front of every person in his outfit and tell them his policies, standards, and goals. He should visit each subunit personally. He should never tell an outfit that it's screwed up. If he does it will be screwed up. Why? Because the boss said so. If a unit is below standard they know they are—in which case the boss should simply tell them after doing his homework that it is good in certain areas but needs to improve in other areas—which *will* happen. Concurrently he should be learning about all of his responsibilities and what each of his subordinate units is charged with accomplishing and a status report on each—and on the boss of each.

Over a ten-day period I flew my helicopter to each of the division camps in South Korea and talked for fifteen minutes or so to every unit. Since the biggest problem facing me, and the reason I was sent to command the 7th Division, was the highly flammable racial situation, my top priority was to get that cooled down and under control. My principal message was that I would see to it that every man was treated fairly and it was up to each man to rise as far as his abilities would take him.

To deal with the racial problem, I first had to get the facts on the scope of the problem. I knew if there were perceptions of unfairness and racial discrimination then those perceptions had to be dealt with just as carefully as real problems and with just as high a priority.

I quickly located the units and the camps with problems and promptly took corrective actions with commanders and with troublemakers, whether white, black, or brown. Many were sent home to the United States and discharged from service.

Early on it was clear to me that many of the race relations problems, and perceptions and real cases of discrimination, occurred at the small-unit level. As I checked into that, other small-unit leadership deficiencies came to light. So we picked some good, experienced officers and senior sergeants and created an Officer's Leadership School for lieutenants and captains and an NCO school for noncoms up through squad leader—each a week long, Sunday through Saturday. Our instructors were carefully chosen from across the division. I taught a couple of classes myself. These schools went a long way toward reducing the racial and drug-abuse problems.

Acting on experience and from past study of successful commanders, I instituted really tough day and night training; off-duty high school and college classes for credit; and all kinds of athletic team competitions. We won the 8th Army boxing and football trophies. Bus trips to historic Korean War battlefields were organized. High standards of individual and unit discipline were established and enforced. Over the months, the division passed with high marks all inspections by very demanding, tough teams from the Pentagon, Far East Command, and 8th Army. I placed great emphasis on discipline and confidence.

I had two principal advisers. One was Col. Jack Bishop. He was a three-war Parachute Infantry veteran who began his military service in the California National Guard as a private, age sixteen. He'd risen through the ranks, knew all the moves, had heard all the stories, and experienced most of the problems. He had four combat jumps in World War II and one more in Vietnam. He was my chief of staff—dead loyal, dead honest, and very candid.

The other was the senior noncommissioned officer in the division—Command Sgt. Maj. Don Peroddy, a big, tough fireplug of a man who wore a handful of Purple Hearts and Silver Stars from Vietnam. He worked only for me, took orders only from me, and had unlimited access to me day or night. He ran the NCOs of the division; set the standards; checked up on them; and was utterly fearless. My first order to him: "Sergeant Major, I don't want any more problems in the villages around our camps. No more fights. No more problems with the Koreans." He straightened things out fast and kept them straight by putting NCOs in the bars and on the streets working with the military police. Early every morning and late every afternoon, I met with each of those men and we talked about immediate problems, developing situations, and whatever they or I wanted to bring up.

I commanded that Infantry division for a year, and in the late spring of 1971 I was ordered to take command of the

Infantry Training Center and Post of Fort Ord, California. Upon doing so, I immediately asked Army Headquarters in Washington to order Colonel Bishop and Command Sergeant Major Peroddy to Fort Ord also. The Army did so and they were a great help to me there for the next two and a half years. These were years of anti–Vietnam War demonstrations, dissident draftees, and plenty of drug problems.

Shortly after I took command, Jane Fonda and her anti-war Fuck The Army (FTA) demonstrators showed up at the front gate of Fort Ord shouting and demanding entrance. Of course, there would be TV cameras present and I knew they wanted a photogenic confrontation between soldiers with fixed bayonets on their M16s and the flower-power children. I gave instructions that the MPs and civilian gate guards were to stand in front of the gate but there was to be no use of force and no weapons or nightsticks in hand. Not even the most rabid of the demonstrators found much joy in nonconfrontation. The TV cameras left and soon the crowd broke up, furious at our pacifism. Later that day, Ms. Fonda somehow gained entrance and was found in the recreation room of one of my Training Center Barracks talking with new soldiers. My MPs quietly and courteously escorted her off the post.

On another occasion I got wind of a large group of protesters who were headed to the other gate of Fort Ord, which was at the city of Seaside, California. I directed my provost marshal to post the oldest civilian gate guard in front of the closed gate, with orders for him to just stand there silently with his hands folded behind his back. No weapon or nightstick on his belt. He did so and again the protesters were furious but got no joy out of screaming at a man older than their grandfathers. They left soon enough. That time I did have a group of MPs standing by out of sight behind a small hill near the gate in the event of an outbreak of violence. In those years we dealt with many antiwar protests at the Fort Ord gates. It was an interesting time to command an Army post. My primary guidance to the MPs and other troops was always the same: Never overreact. That's another maxim I had learned long before and put to good use. There's even a complementary maxim: Never overreact to an overreaction. You will only be playing into a situation you didn't create, even if the other side is spitting in your face or peeing on your boots, as some of these protesters did to the MPs and gate guards.

Fort Ord was an Infantry Training Center providing Basic and Advanced Army Training mostly for new draftees and a far smaller number of volunteer enlistees. The Army was under heavy criticism in those Vietnam War years and my post, situated in northern California, a veritable hotbed of antiwar tension and protests, was accused of being too harsh in training the draftee soldiers. In order to deal with that criticism I organized frequent tours of the base by civilian community leaders and journalists from San Francisco, Oakland, and other cities in the surrounding area. I let them observe training, see where the troops lived, eat with the troops, even talk with the soldiers privately. I welcomed the reporters in particular and saw to it that they could go anywhere they wanted and talk with anyone on the post. My only guidance was simple: "Don't interfere with training."

While I commanded at Fort Ord the Army changed over from a largely draftee force to the beginning of the "Modern Volunteer Army," and just as swiftly the Army was now being criticized for "going soft" on the new volunteer recruits. To combat this I placed great emphasis on bayonet training, pugil stick combat, long runs with weapons, and tough, strict but fair training by the drill sergeants.

Here are some personal observations on related issues on leadership.

ON STRESS:

I never had a problem with stress in battle, probably because it's normal in that situation. In battle soldiers run on adrenaline, quick reflexes, discipline, and water, water, water. I've served in other duties, especially in the Pentagon, where the pressure and stress level were very high due to the volume of work, long hours, and tight deadlines for decisions involving a lot of money and vast numbers of people. That's normal in that environment as well. It can even be exhilarating when you are working with sharp people. To help control that stress, and stay in shape for field duty, every day during the lunch hour I either went to the Pentagon Athletic Club and got a workout playing handball or, on alternate days, ran the two miles over to the Lincoln Memorial and back. I'm a firm believer that physical fitness aids mental fitness. My wife got used to me coming home after a tough day and telling her I was so tired I was going out for a run. It always refreshed me and cleared my mind to deal with the two briefcases of work I brought home.

PUSH THE POWER DOWN:

In my early years as an Infantry officer, I was a paratrooper in the 11th and 82nd Airborne Divisions, then later an Infantry battalion and brigade commander in the 1st Cavalry Division (Airmobile) in Vietnam. In all those units, when on an operation we would be scattered over large areas and individual decision making was the norm—down to the lowest ranks. Based on that experience, in line units and large staff organizations I have led, my policy was always to push the power down. If a subordinate commander, or staff officer, felt comfortable and qualified to make a decision, he could do so with my authority. If not, he could move it up the chain of command a notch. That provided room for the flowering of a lot of talent in my subordinates. But I made sure that they knew that I alone was responsible for what they did or failed to do. I am convinced that trust and loyalty downward results in better work habits and higher unit efficiency.

That policy also kept a hell of a lot of paperwork off my desk, and gave me more time to think, plan ahead, and create the future. Such a policy requires that you keep your subordinates informed and provide guidance on what's hot, what's not—what has changed with your priorities and policies. I always let them know that while I gave them the power to do the job I also checked up to make sure the job was done and done right.

Constantly Train and Improve:

Whatever the endeavor, the troops in the front lines, the workers in the cubicles on their computers, and the sergeants and middle managers must be trained, mentored, and continually improved in performance of duties. The athletic team or business team with the best players and best leaders nearly always wins.

In military units that I have led I talked briefly to my troops on my first day in command and told them about those principles and policies and then I ordered them to get rid of all second-place trophies and awards in the display case. From now on, I told them, only first-place awards will be given or received in this outfit. From now on we are only interested in winning. Then I made it clear that each of them, doing their duty at their level, was just as important and necessary to accomplishing our mission as I was. So it is in any organization. Those who do the work, whether in the trenches or office cubicles or warehouses, are all absolutely essential to success.

Trust Must Be Earned:

With respect to trust, the person in authority at any level—the boss—does not automatically and immediately become a respected and trusted leader by the people under him. He undergoes an unofficial but important observation process in the first few days or weeks during which his subordinates judge him and decide whether or not he is worthy of their trust. It is something that must be earned. They take a hard look at his actions, attitude, judgment, technical proficiency, honesty, his policies, his fairness, his performance and temperament under stress, and most important, his concern for, loyalty to, and relationships with the people under him. In short, how he serves them. Those characteristics reflect the person within—his principles and values.

The leader sets the tone and attitude for his people, his

team; therefore, it's important to display honesty, firm self-confidence, and unwavering commitment to be the best and to accept nothing less from those under him. Some people are born with that self-assured gene and are naturally confident in their ability to shape the future, make the right decisions, and succeed. But it can be developed in others who don't come by it naturally.

Trust Works Three Ways:

In a truly great business organization, athletic team, or military outfit there has to be trust and it has to work in three directions: People in the ranks must trust their leader. People in the ranks must trust each other to do their particular tasks in sync with all other members of the team. And the leader must inculcate and breed into his or her people a strong conviction that he trusts each of them to do the job and do it well. That last form of downward trust creates in the follower an intense desire to do what his leader trusts him to do and never to lose that trust in him.

Of all the units I have led, my fondest and most poignant memories are of the Infantry battalion I commanded in the furious battle of the Ia Drang Valley in Vietnam that long-ago November in 1965. I lost 79 of my troopers killed, 120 wounded, none missing or prisoner. We killed hundreds, maybe thousands of North Vietnamese soldiers, whose bodies were left on the field. We held our ground.

When I first took command of those American soldiers back at Fort Benning I told them I would do my best and expected the same from each of them; that together we would become the best Air Assault Infantry Battalion in the world. We all believed that and that is what we became. We trusted each other implicitly by the time we found ourselves in hand-to-hand combat in that terrible battle. Together, shoulder to shoulder, we fought and died for each other and paid the price. But we held our ground and, in the end, defeated and drove off a force of over 2,000 well-trained, aggressive enemy.

At times, when the danger was greatest and the losses severe, I had a first sergeant commanding an Infantry company in place of his captain. Out with a trapped and decimated platoon a twenty-one-year-old buck sergeant took command when the lieutenant and two more senior sergeants were killed in less than ten minutes of battle. Every soldier did his best. Had even one of them faltered or failed at a critical moment we might well have all perished in that valley, slaughtered like poor Custer's 7th Cavalry so long before. Every American on that field on those three days was a splendid leader. I know the answer to the question: Where do we get such men? We train them and teach them love and loyalty by example. We demand the very best of them and they willingly give it. I will go to my grave thanking them for the privilege of leading and serving them.

TWELVE

On War

Contrary to the conventional wisdom, there's no one more cautious and conservative when it comes to starting a war than old soldiers and old generals who have spent a career, indeed a lifetime, fighting and commanding in wars and suffering the consequences. In the words of Gen. Ulysses S. Grant: "There never was a time when, in my opinion, some way could not be found to prevent the drawing of the sword."

Joe and I are, by virtue of our ages, creatures of the last half of the twentieth century and the early years of the twenty-first and have felt in full the weight of that old Confucian curse "May you live in interesting times." Our professions—mine as a career Infantry officer and Joe's as a foreign and war correspondent—have ensured that we have more than a passing familiarity with the wars and upheavals that have ensued.

Neither of us is a pacifist; neither a jingoist or a war lover. Most wars are cruel and costly mistakes whose causes are rooted in the failure of diplomacy and poor judgment in national leaders. It is far easier to get into a war than it ever is to get out of one. The outcome is seldom what those who championed a war, any war, envisioned when first the bands began to play and soldiers began to march. No one at the time reckons that war will consume billions or even trillions of dollars that might have been better spent on the real needs of a nation and people. Few foresee the crowding of military cemeteries and military hospitals that are the inevitable consequence of war, along with grief-stricken families who have lost a beloved young man or woman and lives not yet lived.

War is absolutely the last card any national leader should play, and only when every other alternative has been exhausted. If the hand was being played by an old soldier, a war veteran, I can assure you he would guard that war card to the bitter end and play it reluctantly and with the fear and trepidation of experience.

There are tests to be met and questions to be answered before going to war: Is it truly in the interest of our national security? Do the people support such a decision and are they willing to serve in that war and sacrifice for it? Is the military fully prepared, trained, and armed to win that war? Do our military planners have an exit strategy? What of our enemy? Do we understand enough about his culture and history and motivation to fight him intelligently? How long is he prepared to continue the fight? Are we prepared to fight at least that long, plus one day more?

Consider that wily old Vietnamese schoolteacher-general, Vo Nguyen Giap, who began a guerrilla war against the French colonial power with a ragged peasant army at the end of World War II. He analyzed the situation and decided that the only way the French could win was by a long, drawn-out war against him, and yet he knew a modern democratic society does not have the political will to endure a long war. It took nearly nine years but Giap's Viet Minh guerrillas beat the French. When the United States entered the Vietnamese conflict Giap was certain the same analysis guaranteed eventual victory over the newcomers as well. It took another decade of death and destruction but in the end he was right.

The questions above demand answers and careful thought *before* the war drums are sounded and the dogs of war let loose. These times, indeed all times, demand national political leaders who know not only our history but the history of the world and its nations and peoples. We need leaders of principle, courage, character, wisdom, and discipline, and yet we seem trapped by a system of choosing our presidents that pushes those who possess those traits aside in favor of others who look good on television, are skilled at slandering and demonizing their opponents in a campaign, and are able to raise the hundreds of millions of dollars required to ensure election at any cost.

While we are certain there are no good wars, we are not so naive as to believe that there are no necessary wars. The greatest war in the history of mankind, World War II, is the best example of a necessary war. It had to be fought to beat back forces and ideas so malignant and aggressive that they threatened the extinction of entire races and nations and would not be stopped by anything less than total war and total defeat, no matter the cost. That cost between 1939 and 1945 included nations on both sides brought to their knees by war's destruction as well as the deaths of some 60 million human beings.

Even so great a war began as a small affair on September 1, 1939, when the German army attacked neighboring Poland and the world stood by uneasily and did nothing as a smaller nation was overwhelmed and enslaved by a much larger one in a rehearsal of all that was to come.

We Americans have been the most fortunate of people. In our history only our own Revolution, the War of 1812, and the Civil War have actually been fought on our soil. We have, historically, been slow to go to war, and even then only when attacked directly or when our interests were threatened. We entered World War I—which virtually wiped out a generation of British, French, and Germans—only for the final two years. We entered World War II for the final four years and only after being attacked by Japan. Fewer than 300,000 of the 60 million dead were American. The Korean War took the lives of more than 1 million Koreans but fewer than 50,000 Americans died there. In Vietnam it is estimated that more than 1 million died in the ten years of the American war; 58,256 of them were American. In the Persian Gulf War fewer than 300 American troops were killed, many of them by so-called friendly fire—American tanks or Bradley Fighting Vehicles mistakenly targeted and attacked by American warplanes or American helicopter gunships.

Because of this the brutal reality of war for the great

majority of Americans is abstract, almost theoretical. That and the dissolution of the Soviet Union, our great Cold War enemy, which left the United States as the reigning and only superpower, may well have given us the idea that war isn't all that bad a solution to nagging problems in troublesome places, and therein lies great danger. This kind of thinking and some spectacular bad judgment led President George W. Bush and his advisers to turn their backs on the idea that we only go to war when attacked or our national interests are directly threatened, as in the Persian Gulf in 1990–1991, and they declared that we would pursue a new policy of preemptive war. We will no longer wait patiently for clear provocation but strike first to nip a perceived potential problem in the bud. We have, to date, only one case history of preemptive action to study and everything we know about it only underlines and argues the need for extreme caution and answering all those pesky questions before acting.

That case history is the Iraq war. In the fall of 2002, with the Bush administration prematurely celebrating victory in toppling the Taliban government in Afghanistan and putting al-Qaeda terrorists on the run and seemingly hell-bent on invading Iraq, I gave serious thought to the issues and kept coming back to these questions: Why? Why Iraq? Why now? Why us? What do we gain? What are we risking?

With all that Bush and Vice President Dick Cheney and then Defense Secretary Donald H. Rumsfeld were telling the American people, I could find no satisfactory answers to my questions and no good reason to go to war with Iraq. Their new doctrine of preemptive military action ran counter to American principles and American history. With very few exceptions—the war with Mexico in the 1840s and the Spanish-American War in the 1890s come to mind—Americans don't start wars. We have to be pushed into wars. Now we were being pushed into a war by our own elected civilian leaders and the question was still: Why?

I listened carefully to the voices urging us to fight and the reasons they gave for doing so and they just didn't add up. The president was not a man of the world like his father. He seemed to have little knowledge of and little interest in foreign affairs and history, especially the long, violent history of the Middle East. Joe was fond of quoting an old Bengali proverb that seemed to apply equally to this situation: "There are a thousand roads into Bengal but no road out." There was little doubt in my mind that our soldiers and Marines—now a professional all-volunteer military—could again take down the army of Saddam Hussein, much as they did in one hundred hours in the Persian Gulf War. But then what? How would we find the road out of Mesopotamia and how many bodies of American soldiers would line its sides?

My military service began as World War II was ending. My first war was Korea, which began with an American diplomatic mistake when Secretary of State Dean Acheson failed to mention South Korea as one of the places we cared enough about to fight for in a speech the Russians and Chinese heard loud and clear. Korea ended in a draw and cost the lives of 50,000 American troops, some of whom died under my command on bleak, frozen hills with names like Old Baldy and Pork Chop that in the end were worth little or nothing.

My next war was Vietnam, where my battalion had the dubious honor of fighting the first major battle against the regiments commanded by a man who later became my friend. That war dragged on for ten long years and ended with a hasty withdrawal just ahead of defeat. More than 58,000 great young Americans were killed and another 300,000 were wounded, and for what? It was the wrong war, in the wrong place, against the wrong people. Three American presidents were entangled and trapped in that debacle.

Now another war loomed and my antennae quivered. My instincts told me Iraq was another mistake; that another American president was marching us off into the quicksand even as his lieutenants made the rosy and ignorant predictions—which come easily to those who have never worn a uniform and never heard a shot fired in anger—of just how swift and successful it was going to be; how little it would cost us in both lives and money; and how great an achievement it would be to topple a brutal dictator and plant democracy in the heart of a volatile region where it had never flourished before.

Joe worked in Washington covering military and national security affairs. He had just finished a brief one-year tour as a special consultant to Gen. Colin Powell at the State Department. His bullshit detector was quivering even more furiously than my antennae. I told Joe and others that it was my estimation that Iraq was not worth the life of even one American soldier; that we were about to become entangled in yet another war that could only end badly. Even worse, this new adventure of the president and his men would draw troops and resources away from the vital mission of finishing off al-Qaeda and Osama bin Laden—the people who carried out the 9/11 attacks on America and killed more than

3,000 innocent people on our soil—in Afghanistan. If history proved anything it was that you never left unfinished business in Afghanistan. Just ask Alexander the Great or Queen Victoria or Leonid Brezhnev, who all suffered bitter defeat in the bleak mountains and trackless deserts of that wild country.

That was my answer in the fall of 2002 before all this began. It is still my answer in the fall of 2007, when more than 160,000 American troops soldier on in a seemingly endless war in Iraq that has, to date, cost the lives of 4,000 of those troops and left more than 60,000 of them wounded or injured. The short and sweet war the president and his men envisioned six years ago has cost us $500 billion to date, and there are estimates that the true cost if it ended tomorrow may exceed $2 trillion. Even at that it has been fought on the cheap by an Army and Marine Corps far too small for the job at hand, with training and equipment never intended for this kind of war. The deployments of these great young men and women on two, three, and four combat tours in Iraq and Afghanistan have worn them and their families down, just as they have ground down the tanks and Humvees and helicopters and aircraft so vital to their mission.

We are into the sixth year of this unnecessary war and our military is on the verge of breakdown. The demands of Iraq have eaten up our strategic reserves and we now have no forces available to cope with emergencies in a world made far more dangerous and hostile to the United States by Mr. Bush's misadventure. I remember with sorrow how low our Army sank in the wake of the withdrawal from Vietnam and how hard and costly it was to repair and rebuild that Army into the vibrant and competent force that swept Saddam Hussein's Iraqi army out of Kuwait in less than a week in 1991.

Those who brought us to this war with such certainty about how easy and quick it would end should be assigned to write long essays on these words from Erasmus: *Dulce bellum inexpertis* (War is delightful to those who have no experience of it). George W. Bush should have old Erasmus's words carved over the entrance to the planned $500 million Bush Presidential Library in Dallas. War is never easy or cheap. Never. When any political leader thinks of starting one he should first seek advice from those who bear the scars and memories of combat and the wives and children of the fallen who live their lives with forever broken hearts.

In the spring of 2005 I traveled to West Point to make my final address to the Corps of Cadets, sixty years since my own graduation and departure from those brooding gray granite walls that loom over the Hudson River. I thought of the thousands upon thousands of fresh-faced young lieutenants who had the virtues of *Duty, Honor, Country* burned into their hearts in this place before they marched into the pages of history during two long centuries of our nation's wars. I knew that some of the most recent graduates had already returned from Iraq to rest under new white marble tombstones in the West Point Cemetery, and I grieved for them.

In that farewell talk to the Corps, whose ranks filled Eisenhower Hall, I spoke of the hard duty at war that awaited them and of the lessons in leadership distilled from my own years of service and time in combat. I told them that of all the tenets of leadership, the greatest of them all was love—that they must love the soldiers they lead more than self, more than life itself. In a long question-and-answer session following my speech I was asked about Iraq and about then Defense Secretary Rumsfeld. In this place—where cadets live by a code that says they never lie, cheat, steal, or quibble—I was bound to speak the truth as I knew it.

The war in Iraq, I said, is not worth the life of even one American soldier. As for Secretary Rumsfeld, I told them, I never thought I would live long enough to see someone chosen to preside over the Pentagon who made Vietnam-era Defense Secretary Robert McNamara look good by comparison. The cadets sat in stunned silence; their professors were astonished. Some of these cadets would be leading young soldiers in combat in a matter of a few months. They deserved a straight answer.

The expensive lessons learned in Vietnam have been forgotten and a new generation of young American soldiers and Marines are paying the price today, following the orders of civilian political leaders as they are sworn to do. The soldiers and those who lead them will never fail to do their duty. They never have in our history. This is their burden. But there is another duty, another burden, that rests squarely on the shoulders of the American people. They should, by their vote, always choose a commander in chief who is wise, well read in history, thoughtful, and slow—exceedingly slow—to draw the sword and send young men and women out to fight and die for their country. We should not choose for so powerful an office someone who merely looks good on a television screen, speaks and thinks in sixty-second sound bites, and is adept at raising money for a campaign.

If we can't get that part right then there will never be an

end to the insanity that is war and the unending suffering that follows in war's wake—and we *must* get it right if we are to survive and prosper as free Americans in this land a million other Americans gave their lives to protect and defend.

EPILOGUE

The Ia Drang brothers in arms and the families of many of those who fell in our battles still gather each year on Veterans Day in Washington, D.C., and in smaller gatherings around the country of veterans of particular units.

In 2005 for the fortieth anniversary of the battles we pulled out all the stops and some 1,200 Ia Drang veterans, families, friends, and supporters came together for a celebration and dinner in the nation's capital.

These reunions of the brothers are filled with joy, sorrow, and healing but each year, as the years march on, there are a few more familiar faces missing, a few more no longer there to stand up when the roll is called and shout out their name, rank, unit, and where they fought in the Ia Drang.

In the winter of 2007 many of us proudly gathered at the White House to see President George W. Bush hang the blue ribbon and gold medallion of the nation's highest award for heroism above and beyond the call of duty around the neck of one of our own, Lt. Col. Bruce Crandall, Ancient Serpent Six. The same president had hung the same medal around the neck of Crandall's wingman and good buddy, Maj. Ed "Too Tall to Fly" Freeman, six years before. Another president, Lyndon B. Johnson, had awarded the Medal of Honor to then Lt. Joe Marm in 1966.

Our story—once almost lost to history—has been told in a best-selling book and a widely acclaimed movie and in countless documentaries and feature articles in a hundred hometown newspapers. Surely, some ask, the passage of the years and the recognition of your deeds in battle have brought closure and healing and peace to all of you? Would that this were true but it is not.

The memories of young men dying and suffering and killing in the horror of hand-to-hand combat in the tall elephant grass under the burning tropical sun are as fresh in our minds as yesterday. Just ask Bill Beck or Clinton Poley or Jon Wallenius or any of us. Ask those who lost a loved one in that valley—ask Barbara Geoghegan Johns or Col. Glen Kennedy or Delores Diduryk—if time really heals all wounds.

We think of our fallen comrades, forever young as we grow old, and of how they died before they had even begun to live. We were all young then and had no real understanding then of all they would never know—the joy of a good woman's love, of watching our children grow, of savoring all that is good and bad in a long life. We who were fortunate enough to survive have tasted all those experiences and now we know all that they gave up when they laid down their precious lives for us. Far from fading in memory, the pain and sorrow only grow more acute.

We are reminded of the words of an old friend and comrade, the late Capt. B. T. Collins, who came home from Vietnam missing an arm and a leg: "We are the fortunate ones! We survived when so many better men all around us gave up their precious lives so that we might live. We owe them a sacred obligation to use each day to its fullest potential, working to make this world a better place for our having lived and their having died."

We are invited to speak at West Point and the Naval Academy and the Air Force Academy and the military service schools and to individual units of today's Army and Marine Corps, and we almost always say yes because we feel an obligation to give something back to our country and our troops in a time when we are, again, at war and these young men and women will be fighting that war and other wars. We owe that to this new generation of warriors just as we owe it to our fallen comrades.

Each of us, in his own way, continues to serve our country because We Are Soldiers Still. . . .

APPENDIX

Two Heroes for America

Two of the most beloved members of the Ia Drang fraternity—one a battlefield hero, the other a home-front hero—are recently gone and their leaving has left empty places in our hearts that can never be filled. One was a big burly Englishman who took great joy from finding the love of his life near the end of his life, and from mortal combat and poetry and the study of the world's religions. The other was a petite woman who was an Army daughter, an Army wife, and an Army mother whose moment of trial arrived with the flood of telegrams announcing a death in battle to Army families in a small southern Army town in Georgia in the fall of 1965. She followed in the wake of the yellow cabs delivering that terrible news and comforted the grieving wives and children of soldiers who fell in the Ia Drang Valley under command of her husband. She helped persuade the Army to change its casualty notification procedures and establish a strong family support system for the future.

Cyril R. "Rick" Rescorla, the finest platoon leader I ever saw in action during two wars, died as he lived—a hero saving lives—on September 11, 2001, at the World Trade Center in New York. My beloved wife, Julia Compton Moore, died on April 18, 2004, in a hospice in Auburn, Alabama, comforted by her children and grandchildren and mourned by thousands of veterans and their families who counted her a close friend and were warmed and comforted by her smile.

It was just past 8:46 a.m. on 9/11. The chief of security for Morgan Stanley Brokerage stood at the window of his office on the forty-fourth floor of Building Two of the World Trade Center in New York. The nightmare he had so accurately predicted eight years before had come true: Terrorists had flown an airliner into Building One just across the way. Plumes of smoke belched from the blazing skyscraper. The squawk box that connected him to the Port Authority Police advised him to keep all his people—2,700 on twenty-two floors of Building Two and another 2,000 in Building Five across the street—at their desks. There's no need to panic, the authorities told him.

"Bugger that!" was his response in the slang of his native England. He grabbed a bullhorn and began working his way down, floor by floor, ordering Morgan Stanley's huge staff to immediately evacuate the building and once they hit the streets to run, not walk, toward safety. Rick Rescorla, who had been a larger-than-life hero all his sixty-two years of living, was just doing what came natural to him: taking care of everyone in sight. We had known him as 2nd Lt. Rick Rescorla, platoon leader in Bravo Company of the 2nd Battalion 7th U.S. Cavalry in both the big battles in the Ia Drang Valley and in a score of other battles in 1965 and 1966 across the Central Highlands. It was his company that was airlifted into LZ X-Ray to reinforce us late on the first day of battle. Bravo Company had been held in reserve until the second day of battle, when I ordered them to replace the battered remnants of my Charlie Company on the southeast side of the landing zone.

Rick was the finest platoon leader I had ever seen in combat and his company commander, Capt. Myron Diduryk, was the finest at his job as well. We joked, proudly, that they were the 1st Cavalry's Foreign Legion. Diduryk was born in Ukraine and came to America as a young boy after World War II. Rescorla was born and grew up in the little tin-mining and seaport town of Hayle in Cornwall in southwest England. That night, after they had tightened the perimeter and shortened the defense lines and dug new, deeper fighting holes and were waiting in the darkness for the attack they knew was coming, Rescorla slipped from hole to hole talking to his men. When spirits were lowest he even sang to them—Old Cornish and Welsh mining tunes and British army songs from the Zulu Wars. He lent them strength from his own fearless heart.

His troops and those of Bravo Company's other platoons drove off four consecutive human wave attacks before the sun came up on November 16, 1965, at a cost of five Americans lightly wounded. The bodies of over 200 North Vietnamese soldiers were piled around their fighting holes and in the tall elephant grass out front.

Later in the morning Rick led the final push to clear the perimeter of the last enemy snipers roped into the trees and hiding behind the termite hills. It is a photograph of Rick Rescorla snapped on that final push that graces the cover of our book *We Were Soldiers Once . . . and Young.* The young lieutenant holding his M16 rifle with bayonet fixed, dirty, unshaven, and weary is captured in a classic Infantry lieutenant's "Follow Me" pose.

Later that day Bravo Company evacuated X-Ray with my 1st Battalion troops, leaving the rest of the 2nd Battalion behind, along with the 2nd Battalion 5th Cavalry. Rescorla and his men were headed for some hot chow and hot showers and clean uniforms back at Camp Holloway in Pleiku. But their break was all too brief. The 2nd Battalion 7th Cavalry walked into an ambush near a clearing called LZ Albany and by nightfall on November 17 were surrounded and fighting for their lives. The brigade commander, Col. Tim Brown, ordered Bravo Company to go to the rescue. They were lifted by helicopter from Holloway to Albany, in a daring night insertion under fire. They had to jump ten feet into the darkness from the hovering choppers. Rescorla strode into the perimeter shouting: "Good. Good. Good. We've got them surrounded now!" He was not only a breath of fresh air but the symbol of new life and strength for men sheltering in shallow fighting holes and crawling to avoid the enemy snipers, if they had to move at all.

Before the fighting was done this battalion and its reinforcements suffered 151 men killed in action, some 130 wounded, and another 4 missing in action whose bodies would not be recovered until April of the following year. As he helped police the bloody battleground the following morning Rescorla retrieved a battered old French army bugle from the body of a North Vietnamese soldier. It was dated before the turn of the century, and had been crudely marked with Chinese characters by its new owners, who had captured it at Dien Bien Phu or in some other desperate last-ditch battle that ended badly for its original owners. Now it belonged to the Cavalrymen of Rescorla's platoon and, in the months following Ia Drang, they would signal their attacks by blowing that bugle in many another battle across the Central Highlands and on the broad coastal plains of the Bong Son.

Rick earned a righteous Silver Star for his actions in both battles, and earned the admiration and respect of all those around him. Awestruck comrades would tell and retell the story of how, early in 1966, Rick and a few volunteers were doing a high-risk reconnaissance mission in the hills above the Bong Son Plain on Vietnam's central coast. They were checking out an abandoned village when Rick stepped through a door and interrupted a dozen or more North Vietnamese soldiers at a meeting. Rick blurted out to the startled enemy troops: "Oh, I beg your pardon," fired off a burst from his M16 rifle, and then ran like the wind for the cover of the jungle with the North Vietnamese in hot pursuit.

Rescorla was no stranger to soldiering and war by the time he landed in the United States and enlisted in the U.S. Army. He had served in the British army on Cyprus and with the Rhodesian police fighting Marxist guerrillas in Africa, and had briefly been a member of Scotland Yard's Flying Squad. But his native England had run out of wars to fight and he found police work boring, so Rescorla came to America in

1963, when the coming war in South Vietnam was little more than a rumor. He was looking for action and he found it. He was tapped to attend Infantry Officer Candidate School (OCS) at Fort Benning, Georgia, in Officer Candidate Class 52 in 1965. That class would become the most decorated group ever to pass through what Army officers call the "Benning School for Boys," with the Medal of Honor recipient Lt. Joe Marm and Rescorla himself leading the way, both of them soon to see combat in the Ia Drang.

Rescorla did only one tour in Vietnam and left active duty in the Army in 1966. He thought that the leadership in Washington, D.C., was looking at this war through rosy-hued glasses and, by dismissing the Vietnamese enemy as no more than a small cog in the wheel of monolithic Communism, were seriously underestimating the nationalism that was at the heart of the enemy's dogged attempts to drive the foreigners, first the occupying Japanese, then the French, and now, us Americans, out of their country.

Although he remained an Army Reserve officer for many more years and rose to the rank of colonel before he retired from service, Rescorla was done with Vietnam. In 1966 he raised his right hand and swore the oath of allegiance to become an American citizen. He went to the University of Oklahoma on the GI Bill and earned a bachelor's and a master's degree in literature at the University of Oklahoma, and went on to earn a law degree there as well.

For a time he taught at a university in North Carolina, but it was too tame a life and the pay was too low to suit him. He drifted into security work and eventually wound up at Dean Witter Brokers in New York, and then became vice president for security at Morgan Stanley when those firms merged. In the 1993 terrorist truck bombing of Building Two at the Trade Center, Rick was once again a hero. When there was near-panic among the brokerage employees on one floor and he couldn't get their attention, Rick jumped on a desk and shouted for silence. When he didn't get it he threatened to drop his trousers and moon the terrified crowd. They fell silent and Rescorla then calmly instructed them where the stairwell doors were located and told them to get out of the building. Then he worked his way up and down the building's floors ordering everyone out, not just those people for whom he was responsible. Rescorla was the last man to walk out of the smoke-filled building.

The following week he went to his superiors and told them that the terrorists had failed in their attempt to destroy the building and predicted with eerie accuracy that "they will be back." He recommended that the brokerage house move to New Jersey, where most of its employees lived, and construct a low-rise high-security headquarters building. Impossible, they said. The company had a long-term lease on the space in these two Trade Center buildings. Rescorla then insisted that he be given the authority to run several surprise full-dress emergency evacuation drills each year. There was grumbling and grousing about what they called "Rick's fire drills" and the expense and trouble involved in pulling hundreds of high-powered brokers off their telephones and then making them and all the support staff hike down forty or fifty or sixty flights of stairs.

But on this day, September 11, all that practice—and Rescorla's instinctive judgment that this was no accident but a coordinated terrorist attack—would save thousands of lives. By the time the second hijacked airliner plowed into Building Two most Morgan Stanley employees were already out in the street running for safety and all the rest were in the stairwells on their way down, two by two, using the buddy system just as they had learned from Rick's fire drills. As the building shuddered and the stairwells filled with smoke and even the well trained were on the verge of panic, Rick lifted his bullhorn and sang to them. This time it was "God Bless America," survivors recall, and some of those old mining songs as well.

He found time to use his cell phone to call his new wife, Susan, who was weeping as she sat glued to the television images of the horror. "I don't want you to cry," he told her. "I have to evacuate my people now. If something happens to me, I want you to know that you made my life." The phone went dead. On her television Susan Rescorla saw the collapse of Building Two and ran screaming out into the street in Morristown, New Jersey, where they lived. She was not the only woman to do so on her street and other suburban streets for miles around.

Rick was on his way back up the staircase to make absolutely certain everyone had gotten out. Two of his security people were with him, along with teams of courageous firemen of the New York City Fire Department. The building came down on them and to date no trace has been found of the body of Rick Rescorla. He and nearly three thousand others died in those two buildings—but only six employees of Morgan Stanley, including Rick Rescorla, were among them.

Now, as Paul Harvey likes to say on the radio, here's the rest of the story. Three years before 9/11 Rick had been diagnosed with prostate cancer that had spread to his bones. The doctors told him he had only about six months to live. He had fought the death sentence with conventional cancer treatments, and Chinese herbal remedies suggested by Susan as well, and the cancer was in remission. But the steroids he continued to take had bloated Rick's body and he now weighed nearly 300 pounds. He had written and spoken to close friends about his fears of retirement in a year or two and how it appeared that his life would end without the kind of great and meaningful cosmic event summed up in the Greek word *kairos*. "I have accepted the fact that there will never be a *kairos* moment for me," Rescorla wrote in an e-mail to his old battlefield buddy, battalion surgeon Dr. William Shucart, six days before 9/11. "Just an uneventful Miltonian plow-the-fields discipline . . . a few more cups of mocha grande at Starbucks, each one losing a little bit more of its flavors."

To another friend Rescorla grumbled, "God, look at us. We should have died performing some great deed—go out in a blaze of glory, not end up with someone spoon-feeding us and changing our nappies." Rick Rescorla's *kairos* moment came, and his departure in a blaze of glory as well. He embraced that moment and his duty, just as he had done at age twenty-six on the battlefields of the Ia Drang Valley and just as anyone who knew him expected he would do. He was a warrior prince, a singer of songs, a poet, a writer, a romantic, a father to two children, Trevor and Kim, and our good friend and com- rade. They broke the mold when they made Rick Rescorla. There is no tombstone in Arlington Cemetery with his name engraved on white marble. He told any and all that he didn't want that. There's just a small bronze memorial plaque on an eagle's cage in a wildlife sanctuary called Raptors in New Jersey. That, and a life-size, quite accurate bronze statue of the young lieutenant from that iconic photo taken in Landing Zone X-Ray, which is in the Infantry Museum in Fort Benning, Georgia, where they still turn out Infantry officers and soldiers for America's wars.

Across the Atlantic in Hayle, Cornwall, they collected small donations, little by little from the townsfolk, to build a lovely granite memorial topped with a bronze eagle, in memory of their hero, the boy nicknamed "Tammy" who was the only child of a single mother. Their Tammy is remembered as a brawler and tough competitor in the local rugby football games. He had never forgotten his hardscrabble roots and the hometown folks, and when he came back on trips to visit his mother he always made a point of visiting a lonely old blind man, Stanley Sullivan, at the nursing home. Rick would smuggle in cans of stout and he and Stanley would stay up late drinking and singing tearful renditions of the old Cornish songs.

We who served with him began a petition campaign within weeks after 9/11, urging President George W. Bush to bestow a posthumous award of the Presidential Medal of Freedom on Rick Rescorla. Over 40,000 signatures have been collected to date and many personal appeals have been made to the White House, without either action or response.

His comrades at arms remember one Rick, the tough guy who could be a hard-eyed killer one minute and the life of any party at the tin-roofed homemade officers club back at home base in An Khe. We remember a lieutenant whose radio call sign was Hard Core. The folks of Hayle remember another, the hometown boy. Susan Rescorla remembers still another Rick—the romantic who would suddenly grab her and dance her joyously around the house, the street, or a shop full of strangers. She remembers the poet, the lover, the wood carver, the playwright, the man who could suddenly begin reciting from memory great chunks of Shakespeare or Proust or Milton. She talks of how they had been married for months and she knew nothing of his role in combat in Vietnam or his medals, only that he had been in the Army a long time ago. It was not until she accompanied Rick to the U.S. Military Academy at West Point to attend a lecture I was giving to the Corps of Cadets that Susan found out she was married to a genuine hero.

I introduced Rick to the cadets and told them of his critical part in the fighting in LZ X-Ray and LZ Albany and his superb leadership—something they already knew—and he received a boisterous standing ovation. Afterward Susan watched in amazement as the young cadets lined up by the hundreds to have Rick sign their dog-eared copies of our book and reach out and shake the hand of a true hero and role model. She remembers their first meeting, on a dawn walk with her dog through the streets of Morristown, New Jersey, when Rick jogged by barefooted. He stopped to take a breath and she asked why he had no shoes. Rick told her he was writing a screenplay about Africa and needed to know what it was like to run barefooted, as his characters did. Susan talks of her new husband who took her on a visit to Hayle a year after their marriage and there suggested that they renew their wedding vows outside an ancient, abandoned church, reciting his version of those words that join a man and woman together.

———

Today, in the suburbs of New Jersey and the skyscrapers of Manhattan, there are thousands of men and women who are living their normal lives and doing their normal jobs because of a man named Rick Rescorla. But for him and his sense of duty the death toll at the World Trade Center would be twice as high. No one will ever have to spoon-feed or change the diapers on one particular old veteran in a nursing home. Near the end Rick was studying Zen Buddhism, and if what he read is right, one day he may return to live another life filled with adventure and even greater deeds. His sort are always needed in this world, and somehow they always appear when most needed.

I t was the middle of April 2004, and spring had come to the hills of Alabama and southern Georgia. The wild dogwood and redbud brought color to the woods and the azaleas were in full bloom in well-tended yards.

Drivers on Interstate 85 east of Auburn, Alabama, must have been startled when a phalanx of State Highway Patrol cars, red lights flashing, waved them off the highway and raced ahead to block the entrance ramps that fed into the river of traffic moving east.

Other state troopers and police led a hearse and long black limousines and a convoy of hundreds of other cars onto the interstate. It stretched back a mile and more. Then the cortege turned off the interstate and onto U.S. Highway 280, traveling south and east through the rolling Georgia hills.

Must be some former governor or maybe an old general to receive such an escort, such a cleared path to the cemetery, those sidelined motorists surely were thinking; never seen them block an interstate highway for a funeral procession before. But this honor and tribute was not for a politician or a general or a bishop. It was the final, sad ride home for a true unsung American hero: we were carrying Julia Compton Moore from the home she loved in the sleepy southern college town of Auburn to the old Post Cemetery on the grounds of Fort Benning, Georgia, her final resting place in the arms of what she only half-jokingly called "Holy Mother Army."

Julie's life began and ended with the United States Army and was inextricably bound to that institution for all of her seventy-five years. She was every inch a soldier herself all of those years, as much as, perhaps even more than, the men she loved who wore the Army uniform: her father, husband, and sons.

Her story and her own quiet heroism during five of our country's wars in which those she loved served in combat— World War II, Korea, Vietnam, Panama, and the Gulf War— had been told in our book and in the movie based on that book. In those dark days of November 1965, it was my wife, Julie, who followed the taxi drivers, house to house, trailer park to trailer park, in Columbus, Georgia, as they delivered the telegrams to Army wives and Army children telling them they had lost the one person who mattered most in their lives. It was Julie, the wife of their husband's battalion commander, who came to their door to help them grieve and stood beside them at graves dug in the red earth of a Georgia Army post and helped them say farewell as an Army coffin was lowered into that red earth.

It took all her strength and courage to face those griev-ing women, even as she lived in fear that the next telegram to arrive might carry her name and address. She worried that those families would hate her because it was her husband who had led their men into the battle that took their lives. But there was no hate for a woman who came to share their sorrow; no anger directed toward another Army wife who was doing her duty as she had been taught by her own mother and father, and by her husband, who was now commanding soldiers in his second war.

Her own anger, her own considerable strength and iron will, would now be directed at righting what she considered a huge mistake by the Army she loved: dispatching taxi drivers to deliver the Western Union death notifications to the families of soldiers killed in the Vietnam War. She and the wife of the 1st Cavalry Division commanding general together would lay telephone siege to the Pentagon, demanding that *their* Army do the right thing, right now. Within a matter of weeks Army policy would change. Those terrible telegrams would no longer arrive in the middle of the night and be handed over by a taxi driver. Instead an Army officer and an Army chaplain would personally come to break the news that would break so many hearts.

Just as she was brought home to an Army post at the end of her life, so, too, had she begun that life on another Army post: Julie was born on February 10, 1929, at Fort Sill, Oklahoma, home of the Army Field Artillery, to Captain and Mrs. Louis J. Compton. She was their only child and she was the quintessential Army brat, growing up on Army posts across America during the years between the two great World Wars as her father moved from assignment to assignment in the small, tightly knit Army of that time. She and her mother lived in Washington, D.C., off Reservoir Road in the shadow of Georgetown University, during the years when Colonel Compton was serving overseas in World War II in the European theater. Julie attended and graduated from Chevy Chase Junior College just across the line in Maryland.

Her father in 1948 was assigned to Fort Bragg, North Carolina, and Julie went off to the University of North Carolina at Chapel Hill. In June of that same year I was assigned to the 82nd Airborne Division at Fort Bragg. Julie was visiting her parents there in August of that year when the two of us met. She was nineteen years old, an auburn-haired beauty with an outgoing personality. I burned up the roads between Fayetteville, North Carolina, and Chapel Hill during the next year and a half, courting the woman I knew was meant for me. We were married at Fort Bragg on November 22, 1949, and our wedding reception was held at the old Officers Club on that post.

Our first son, Greg, was born in the spring of 1951 at the Army hospital at Fort Bragg. Our second son, Steve, was born a year later at Martin Army Hospital on Fort Benning. By then I was on orders to deploy to Korea, where the war was raging. Just a month later, in late June, I boarded a plane in Louisville, Kentucky, and left Julie standing there with two babies in her arms. By then her father had retired from the Army and was living in Auburn. Julie and the two babies moved in with the Comptons and lived with them for fourteen months while I was soldiering in Korea.

When I got home Julie resumed the gypsy life she had known as an Army brat, only now as an Army wife and Army mother. Packing up, moving, unpacking, settling in for a year or two years in places like Fort Benning; Fort Myer, Virginia; West Point; Fort Belvoir; Fort Leavenworth; Newport, Rhode Island; Oslo, Norway; Fort Benning again; Korea; Fort Ord, California; then back to Fort Myer. We lived in nine states, two foreign countries, twenty-five different homes, and Julie packed and unpacked our household twenty-four times over the years.

Our daughter Julie was born at West Point in the fall of 1954 and daughter Cecile at Fort Belvoir in the winter of 1958. We were in Norway when Julie gave birth to our third son, Dave, with the help of a Norwegian midwife, in 1961. The two older sons attended a Norwegian Catholic school and rapidly became fluent in Norwegian.

Julie was the rock of our family. On her we built a home rich in love, caring, and tradition. She volunteered as a den mother for the boys, taught sewing and crafts to the girls, and drove them to all the countless activities. She kept the house running amid times of chaos and joy that five growing children present. Never at a loss for song at the spur of the moment, always accurately sensing the mood of a situation, she knew how to instantly lighten our hearts. The Army was her family as well. The love she gave our family was selflessly extended to every community where we were assigned—"Bloom where you are planted," Julie told us. It is this love that she extended to the wives and children of the Army family that would prove invaluable in times of crisis and help me build unit cohesion in times of peace.

The movie *We Were Soldiers*, taking poetic license, wrongly depicted all the wives and families of my battalion living in Army quarters, nice two-story bungalows on Colonel's Row at Fort Benning after we left for Vietnam. That was Hollywood. Like all the other families living in Army quarters when we were ordered to Vietnam in the summer of 1965, Julie and our family of five were given thirty days to vacate those quarters and go somewhere else, anywhere else. The Army didn't particularly care where.

Some of the wives of young officers went home to live with their own families, much as Julie had done during the Korean War. But the wives and children of the senior non-commissioned officers were as bound to the Army as Julie was and they scattered out in a desperate search for housing in Columbus, Georgia, just outside the gates of Fort Benning. For most that meant a rented trailer house in a sun-baked treeless trailer park. In those days it also meant blacks on one side of town, whites on the other. The only house Julie could find for rent was a tiny three-bedroom cottage, and she and the five kids crammed in there and waited for my homecoming. Each night she unfolded a cot for our son David, as there wasn't room for one more bed anywhere.

At every Army post where she lived, from captain's wife to colonel's wife to general's wife, Julie did everything she could to help the families of soldiers. She organized the officers and NCO wives to provide mutual support and worked to develop child-care facilities so that the wives could work and contribute to the pitifully small salaries their husbands earned from the Army. She was expert at whipping out a good, big dinner when I called on short notice and told her I was bringing guests home. She was an extrovert and never met a stranger at any of the official functions. She did all this while juggling all the duties of a mother with five children, and she did it better than anyone I ever heard about. Julie worked as a Red Cross volunteer "gray lady" from the time she was a teenager during World War II. After we married she continued that volunteer work in Army hospitals at Fort Bragg, Fort Benning, Korea, Fort Ord, and Fort Myer, at the U.S. embassy clinic in Oslo, and at the hospital in our hometown of Auburn.

Two of our sons, Steve and Dave, followed my footsteps to West Point and into the Army, and now Julie had given two more hostages to fortune and war. Our son Dave, a paratrooper, made the combat jump into Panama with the 82nd Airborne Division and his mother worried every day until he was home safely. In 1990 Dave, now a captain, was sent with the 82nd Airborne to Saudi Arabia in Operation Desert Shield. War was again looming and again Julie worried about a loved one going in harm's way. In January 1991, on the eve of Desert Storm and the invasion of Iraq and Kuwait by American and coalition forces, Joe got orders to return to Saudi Arabia as we prepared for imminent war. He phoned the house in Auburn to let me know he would be leaving Andrews Air Base outside Washington, D.C., early the next morning and would be out of touch for a while. I wasn't home so he gave the message to Julie. She told him, "Joe, I am so worried about this war and son Davey being right in the middle of it." Joe responded with surprise, saying that she had sent her father and her husband off to other wars and surely she was used to this by now. Julie's response was swift and to the point: "Joe Galloway, you don't understand one damn thing about this. You can replace a husband but you can never replace a son!"

Dave made it through the Persian Gulf War okay and remains on duty in our Army today. In the fall of 2006, I pinned his grandfather's silver eagle on one shoulder and my own colonel's eagle on the other as he was promoted at Fort Monmouth, New Jersey. His mom would have been so proud, and so worried about his trips to Iraq in yet another war.

After I retired from the Army in 1977 we moved to Crested Butte, Colorado, where for a time I managed the ski resort there for former Secretary of the Army Bo Callaway. Julie set up yet another home for us just down the road from the ski lifts on Mount Crested Butte. But her heart remained in Auburn, in the home she inherited from her mother and father when they died, where she lavished loving attention on the banks of azaleas that were her pride and joy when they burst into fiery bloom in the Alabama springtime. After I left the job at the ski resort we divided our time between our two homes, moving back and forth two or three times each year. Julie's Army training in the art and skills of packing and moving stood her in good stead.

When they were preparing to film *We Were Soldiers* she entertained the stars, Mel Gibson and Sam Elliott and Madeleine Stowe, at our home and she was not shy in giving her advice to writer-director Randall Wallace. She was outraged when she discovered that all of the actresses chosen to play the Army wives of 1965 were white women. The wives she worked with and grieved with were, like the Army itself, of every race and creed. When she followed those taxicabs to the trailer parks of Columbus she went into the homes of black women, Hispanic women, and Native American women as well as white women, and she wanted that truth to be reflected in this film.

She won that battle but lost others to the "artistic license" that Hollywood insisted on as its due. Julie wanted the people who saw this movie to see the women and children crammed into those little trailer houses all around Columbus, not living the life of Riley in spacious two-story homes on Colonel's Row at Fort Benning. She wept bitter tears over the battles she lost, but Julie Moore did her dead-level best to make that movie as true to life—the lives of those who waited for their men to come home—as humanly possible.

In the early spring of 2002 she joined us as the film premiered in Hollywood, at the White House, and even better yet at Fort Benning, Georgia, and Fort Hood, Texas, by then the home base of the 1st Cavalry Division. She became a close friend of the actress Madeleine Stowe, who portrayed her in that movie. The fame that came from first the book and then the movie made no real difference in the life of Julie Moore. She typed my e-mails and letters, just as she had typed my contributions to both the book and movie. She still whipped up dinner for surprise guests, and fielded phone calls from my troopers and the families of those she had comforted in their terrible loss so many years before. She and four old friends still gathered one afternoon a week in Auburn to play bridge.

But in late February 2004 Julie fell ill with a rare and deadly form of cancer. Julie fought it with every bit of determination she had always brought to every battle, every challenge in her life. My beloved wife of fifty-five years, my lover, my strong right arm, died on the morning of April 18, 2004, just six weeks after her diagnosis. Julie always had a positive attitude in dealing with the setbacks, adversities, and accidents of daily life. When confronted with bad news her response was always: "My father told me early in life that you are a

Compton, and Comptons are thoroughbreds, and thorough-breds don't cry."

I was beside her in the doctor's office in Auburn when he told her that her cancer was incurable. She took that terrible news quietly. I was with her at the M. D. Anderson Hospital in Houston, Texas, when the doctor told her she would die soon. She asked him: "How long do I have—a month . . . more . . . less?" The doctor said she had perhaps one week. She nodded and said simply: "I'm a thoroughbred and thorough-breds don't cry. . . ." She wanted to go home to Auburn and the next day an air ambulance with a nurse aboard brought her home and to the hospice there. She had just four days left to live. Her fight with cancer, the same small cell (oat cell) cancer that eight years before had taken the life of Joe's wife of thirty years, Theresa Null Galloway, was one of the few battles Julie Moore ever lost. This cancer is not specific to any particular organ. Theresa's was believed to have begun in the small intestine; Julie's began in one of her lungs, even though she had quit smoking two decades before. Wherever it begins, this cancer is very aggressive and migrates swiftly all over the body. In the cases of both Theresa and Julie there was only six weeks between diagnosis and death. The night before she died Joe sat beside Julie's bed in the hospice. With all five of her children standing by she roused and whispered: "Oh, Joe. We've come so far together, and we still have so far to go."

Now she was going home to rest in the arms of her Army, just a few feet from where her mother and father were buried. The Post Cemetery at Fort Benning was filled to capacity with the small white marble markers over the graves of hundreds of soldiers and the wives of soldiers. There was no place for Julie

Compton Moore, soldier's daughter, soldier's wife, soldiers' mother. No place until the widow of Sgt. Jack Gell, one of my troopers in Alpha Company who was killed on the first day of the battle at Landing Zone X-Ray, graciously gave up a place she had long ago reserved for herself next to her husband.

The Catholic church in Auburn was filled to overflowing for her service. Then that mile-long convoy wound its way along Interstate 85 and then on U.S. 280 for the last twenty-six miles to Fort Benning. Although every American military base was still on high alert in the wake of 9/11, the gates of Fort Benning swung wide open as Julie Moore came home. There were generals and colonels and a former governor of Alabama there to see her off, but most of all there were former sergeants and former specialists and former privates, and there were some of the widows and children of men whose funerals she had attended in this same cemetery so many years before.

If ever there was a civilian who had earned a full-dress military funeral with a flag-draped coffin and a firing party of soldiers and a bugler to blow the bittersweet notes of Taps it was Julie Moore. But the Army has rules and regulations and there was none of that military pomp when we laid Julie to rest next to Sergeant Gell, amid the graves of my fallen troopers, a few rows down from Colonel and Mrs. Compton.

We were married for fifty-five years and were more in love at the end of those years together, I think, than we were in the beginning. When I think of my Julie, which is every single day, I think of what it says in the Bible, Proverbs 31:10–12: "A good wife is far more precious than jewels. The heart of her husband trusts in her and he will have no lack of gain. She brings him good and not harm, all the days of her life." I visit the Fort Benning Post Cemetery often now to talk to Julie and walk the rows of those white tombstones that mark the last resting place of some of my troopers, who gave the last measure of devotion to this country in battle. I'm eighty-six years old and will join them all soon enough. Then we will all rest together, in the arms of Holy Mother Army.

ACKNOWLEDGMENTS

Our thanks, as always, go first to our friends who fought in or provided valuable support in the Ia Drang battles, as well as the families of those who fell there. No one ever had finer or more loyal comrades.

A special thank-you is due those who shared with us the remarkable journey back to Vietnam and back to the Ia Drang that is at the heart of the story told in this book: CSM (ret.) Basil L. Plumley, Lt. Col. (ret.) Bruce Crandall, Col. (ret.) Tony Nadal, Col. (ret.) John Herren, former Capt. S. Lawrence Gwin Jr., Lt. Col. (ret.) George Forrest, former Sgt. Ernie Savage, former Sp. 4 Bill Beck, and the late Jack Smith.

What made the journey back to the battlefields special was the company of three remarkable old soldiers of the

North Vietnamese People's Army who had fought us there as wartime enemies but joined us in a search for peace. So we thank: the late Lt. Gen. Nguyen Huu An, who was the NVA commander on the battlefield, and two of his comrades, Col. Tran Minh Hao and Col. Vu Dinh Thuoc.

The journey would never have happened without a young ABC-TV producer named Terry Wrong, who read our first book and made the proposal to take us back to Vietnam and back to the battlefields for a one-hour documentary for the network's *Day One* program. Terry sold the idea to his bosses and then to us. So thanks to Terry Wrong, correspondent Forrest Sawyer, and their able assistant and interpreter Miss Quynh Thai, who joined us on the trip along with a four-man camera and sound crew. The resulting documentary, titled *They Were Young and Brave*, earned well-deserved awards and honors for Terry.

Our official host in Vietnam was, again, the Foreign Press Service and our old friend, former director Nguyen Cong Quang. He provided us an excellent translator, Vu Binh, who was with us every step of the way.

Our gratitude and thanks also to Col. (ret.) James Pritzker, the Tawani Foundation, and the Pritzker Military Library of Chicago for their encouragement and support during the writing of this book.

Mr. and Mrs. Toby Warren of Auburn, Alabama, earn special mention for their friendship and daily support of this project as the strong right arms for Hal Moore. They offered a thousand favors, large and small, and did a multitude of chores out of love and respect.

We owe heartfelt thanks to our agent, Mel Berger of the

ACKNOWLEDGMENTS

William Morris Agency in New York, and to his assistant, Evan Goldfried, as well as to our editors at HarperCollins, who made this a much better book by their hard work— Alison Callahan, Doug Grad, and Kate Hamill.

Last, but certainly not least, our love and thanks to our children, who have put up with the burden of having their dads working on a book and thus totally distracted and absentee parents twice now in fifteen years. This is for Greg, Steve, Julie, Cecile, and David Moore, and Lee and Joshua Galloway.

An Appeal

We believe that the beginning of an end to war has to lie in higher education and, toward that end, we established the Ia Drang Scholarship Fund under the auspices of the 1st Cavalry Division Foundation to provide college assistance for the sons and daughters of all who participated in or supported the American troops in the Ia Drang battles.

This Fund has been expanded to include the grandchildren of Ia Drang veterans and provides a check each year for dozens of eligible young men and women to further their education.

If the stories told in our two books about the soldiers and the battles have moved the reader to reach out, we would urge that you make a tax-deductible contribution to the Fund to ensure that it lives on after we are gone.

AN APPEAL

Such contributions, payable to 1st Cavalry Div. Foundation (Ia Drang), should be mailed to:

1st Cavalry Division Foundation
302 N. Main Street
Copperas Cove, TX 76522

Lt. Gen. Hal Moore
Joe Galloway

INDEX

ABC television, 5, 22, 41, 48, 63,
      86, 95, 99, 155,   228
Acheson, Dean, 192
Adams, Russell, 92–94
Afghanistan, xvi, 191, 194
Alexander the Great, 194
Alley, Lt. Bud, 67
al-Qaeda, 193–94
American Graffiti II (film), 15
An, Lt. Gen. Nguyen Huu, 33,
      122, 228
   accounts of ambush by, 12–13
   background of, 49, 68–69
   in Cambodia, 68
   commander, Ia Drang, 4, 11,
      21, 35, 37, 53, 68, 91, 92
   death and funeral, 142–44, 149
   defense against Chinese invad-
      ers and, 69
   at Dien Bien Phu, 33, 68, 133,
      142
   learns truth about his opponent
      at LZ Albany, 38–39
   meeting with, 1991, 38–39
   Moore's friendship with, 68,
      69, 98–99
   return to Ia Drang (1993),
      48–49, 53, 64, 84, 96, 98,
      109–10, 113, 148–49

An Khe base, 13, 64–67, 68, 212
   Garry Owen Officers Club, 67
   Army War College, Carlisle,
      Pennsylvania, 93–94
Associated Press (AP), 55

B-52 bombers, 11, 36, 39
Bai, Mr., 24–25, 26–27
Ball, George, 32
Baptism (Gwin), 63–64
Barker, Oscar, Jr., 119
Beck, Bill, 42, 47, 50–51, 92–94,
      96, 104–5, 200
Bell UH-1 Iroquois (Huey), 15
   in air assault, Ia Drang, 5, 7, 8,
      9, 10, 87, 133
   assigned to 3rd Brigade, Air
      Cavalry, 6
   command helicopter, Ia Drang,
      9
   evacuating LZ X-Ray, 10
   No. 63-8808, disappeared Dec.
      28, 1965, 87
Bengali proverb, 192
Binh, Vu, 99, 109, 228
bin Laden, Osama, 193–94
Bishop, Col. Jack, 178, 179
Bonebrake, Master Sergeant,
      73–74

INDEX

Brezhnev, Leonid, 194
Bright Shining Lie, A (Sheehan), 32
Brokaw, Tom, 151
Brown, Col. Tim, 6, 123, 206
Burnite, Barry, 119, 121
Burns, Ken, 155
Bush, George H. W., 27
Bush, George W., 152, 212–14
    awarding of Congressional
        Medal of Honor to Crandall,
        200
    failure of judgment, 191–92
    Iraq War as mistake, 193–97
    lack of war experience, 195
    Presidential Library in Dallas,
        195

C-123, 63, 77
Cambodia, 2, 3, 4, 5, 10, 68, 97
Camp Holloway, Pleiku, 3, 6, 10,
    122, 123, 206
Caravelle Hotel, Saigon, 150–51
Carrerra, Robert, 78
Catecka Tea Plantation, Brigade
    Headquarters, 9
Chandler, A. B. "Happy," 158,
    159–60
Cheney, Dick, 191
China, 151
    Communism/Communists in, 2
    human-wave tactics, 45
    Korean War and, 131–32, 138
    trade with Vietnam, 151–52
    Vietnam War and, 132
Chu Dreh Pass, 147–48
Civil War, 190
    Pickett's Charge, 171
Clinton, Bill, 27
Collins, Capt. B. T., 201
Communism/Communists
    death of, 2, 43
    in Vietnam, 2, 43, 151–52

Compton, Captain and Mrs. Louis
    J., 216–17, 224
Congressional Medal of Honor,
    xvii, 200
Continental Hotel, Saigon, 151
Cox, Eugene E., 160
Crandall, Maj. Bruce, xvii, 3, 10,
    42, 47, 61, 63, 78, 86–87,
    200, 227
Creal, Ed, 160, 161
Crittenden, Jules, 116–18
Cronkite, Walter, 151
Custer, Col. George Armstrong,
    8–9, 67, 185

Dang, Minh Van, 99
Day One (TV program), 5, 22, 41,
    42, 228
de Castries, Brig. Gen. Christian,
    134–36, 140
Diduryk, Capt. Myron, 205
Diduryk, Delores, 200
Dien Bien Phu, 22, 31, 33, 34, 42,
    44–47, 67, 85, 132, 133–42
    casualties, 130, 140
    French prisoners taken, 140
    French strongpoints, naming of,
        139, 141–42
    lessons of, 130, 132–33
    studies of, 129
    today, 139–40
Dillon, Capt. Greg "Matt," 9, 79,
    171
Drucker, Peter, 166

Eade, Sgt. John, 118–21
Edwards, Capt. Bob, 106
8th Army, 173, 177–78
82nd Airborne Division, 76, 217,
    220
11th Airborne Division, 76
Elliott, Sam, 76–77, 221

Erasmus, 195
Esper, George, 55–56
Evans, Harry, 17

F-100 fighters, 107
Fall, Bernard, 129
5th Cavalry
    5th Cavalry, 1st Battalion, 42,
        113
    5th Cavalry, 2nd Battalion, 11,
        206
1st Cavalry Division, 3, 6, 11, 15,
        29, 31, 36, 63, 65, 149
    Airmobile, 3, 28, 123, 182
    3rd Battalion, 6
    3rd Brigade, 12, 13, 62, 78–79
    Hueys available to, 6, 28
1st Cavalry Division Foundation,
        229–30
Fonda, Jane, 179
Forrest, Lt. Col. George, 42, 47,
        50–51, 99, 103, 110, 113,
        115, 121, 124, 227
Fort Belvoir, 218
Fort Benning, Georgia, 6, 47, 74,
        76, 106, 184, 208, 218, 219,
        220, 223–24
    cemetery, 223–24, 225
    Infantry Museum, 212
    Martin Army Hospital, 47, 80,
        217
Fort Bragg, North Carolina, 217, 220
Fort Leavenworth, 218
Fort Monmouth, New Jersey, 221
Fort Myer, Virginia, 218, 220
Fort Ord, California, 178–81, 218,
        220
Fort Sill, Oklahoma, 216
France
    Americans' contempt for French
        fighters, 130
    cemetery in Vietnam, 67

colonialism of Indochina, 22,
        25, 60, 189
end of rule in Indochina, 22,
        30, 44, 45, 68, 133 (see also
        Dien Bien Phu)
Groupe Mobile 100 in Korea,
        67
Indochina War (see Indochina
        War)
influence on Vietnamese cul-
        ture, 60
public pressure to end Indo-
        china War, 135
Freeman, Capt. Ed, xvii, 200
Fuck the Army (FTA), 179

Galloway, Joseph L., 93–94
    battle at Ia Drang, xviii, 9–10,
        78, 107
    Bengali proverb, 192
    career post-Vietnam, xviii,
        14–17
    confrontation with Gen.
        Knowles, 123
    desire to talk with North Viet-
        namese commanders, 20–21
    evolution of book, 14–17,
        101–2
    friendship with Col. Thuoc,
        144–45
    Iraq War and, 193–97
    in Jakarta, 59
    Julia Moore's death and, 223
    Man and, 144
    meets Giap, 31–33, 44–47, 130
    meets Moore, 9–10
    National Magazine Award,
        16–17
    night on battlefield (1993), 99,
        102–3, 105
    Persian Gulf War and, xi, xviii,
        17, 220

Galloway, Joseph L. *(cont.)*
  Plumley and, 6, 7, 77–78,
    88–89, 95
  reports on battle at LZ X-Ray,
    10
  reports on Vietnam War, 14
  return to Ia Drang (1993), 1–4,
    22, 41–69, 86, 96, 147–51,
    155
  return to Pleiku (1993), 83–86
  return to Vietnam (1990),
    15–16, 20–33
  return to Vietnam (1991), 22,
    33–40
  return to Vietnam (1999), 22,
    130, 134–45
  return to Vietnam (2005), 22,
    153–54
  Schwarzkopf and, xii
  U.S. News & World Report cover
    article on Ia Drang, 2, 5
  visit to An's widow, 142–44
  visit to Dien Bien Phu (1999),
    130
  war, beliefs about, 187–88
  weapons carried by, 10, 31, 78
  wife's death, 223
Galloway, Joshua, 229
Galloway, Lee, 229
Galloway, Theresa Null, 223
Gell, Sgt. Jack, 224
Geoghegan, Lt. Jack, 106, 200
  family of, 106
George Washington University,
  159
Giap, Gen. Vo Nguyen, 16, 30, 33,
  42, 130, 134, 142, 189
  at Dien Bien Phu, 22, 42,
    44–47, 130–31, 135, 138,
    140–41
  meeting with, 1990, 21, 25,
    30–33

  meeting with, 1993, 44–47
  meeting with, 1999, 22
  thirtieth anniversary of fall of
    Saigon and, 154
Gibson, Mel, 221
Godboldt, PFC Willie, 106
Grant, Gen. Ulysses S., 187
Greene, Graham, 151
Grella, Don, 87
Gwin, Lt. Larry (later Capt.), 42,
  47, 63–64, 67, 96, 99, 102,
  105, 109, 113, 115, 121,
  122, 227
  C-123 crash and, 63

Hanoi, 2, 49, 20–33
  B-52 bombing raids, Christmas,
    1972, 40
  building and corruption in,
    152
  changes and growth, 42–43,
    152, 154
  dikes, 152
  Hotel Metropole, 51
Hao, Col. Tran Minh, 53, 91, 96,
  97, 109–10, 122, 126–27,
  149, 228
helicopters, 6, 28. *See also* 1st Cavalry Division (Airmobile)
  Bell UH-1 Iroquois (Huey), 5, 7,
    8, 9, 10, 15, 87, 133
  first deployment, Ap Bac
    (1962), 31–32
  NVA reaction to, 29
  Soviet-made Hind, 2–3, 86, 89,
    99, 110, 113
  229th Assault Helicopter Bat-
    talion, 10
Hell in a Very Small Place (Fall),
  129
Herren, Capt. John (later Col.), 7,
  8, 42, 47, 90, 97, 227

Hmong tribes, 152
Ho Chi Minh, 30, 31, 135
Ho Chi Minh Trail, xv, 4, 22, 28, 37, 85, 136
"How to Fight the Americans" (Phuong), 29
Huey. *See* Bell UH-1 Iroquois (Huey)
Hussein, Saddam, xviii–xix, 195

Ia Drang Scholarship Fund, 229–30
Ia Drang Valley, battles of, xv–xvi, 7–13
   1st Cavalry Division (Airmobile), 11
   5th Cavalry, 1st Battalion, 42, 113
   5th Cavalry, 2nd Battalion, 11, 206
   7th Cavalry, 1st Battalion, Alpha (A) Company, 8, 38, 41–42
   7th Cavalry, 1st Battalion, Bravo (B) Company, 7, 10, 38, 42, 96
   7th Cavalry, 1st Battalion, Charlie (C) Company, 78, 96, 105–6, 172–73
   7th Cavalry, 2nd Battalion, 11–13, 39, 42, 122, 206
   7th Cavalry, 2nd Battalion, Alpha (A) Company, 63, 64, 113, 118
   7th Cavalry, 2nd Battalion, Bravo (B) Company, 77, 90–92, 205–7
   7th Cavalry, 2nd Battalion, Charlie (C) Company, 86, 113, 124, 125
   ABC television documentary, 5, 22, 41–42, 63, 95–96, 115, 155, 228

air support, fighter-bombers, U.S., 9, 11, 36
An's command post, 38, 39
B-52 bombers sent to saturate Chu Pong Massif, 11, 36
   as bloodiest battle in Vietnam War, xvi
   casualties, American, xv, xvi, 3, 9, 12, 17, 90, 91, 101–2, 106, 108–9, 115, 116, 123, 124, 172–73, 184, 200, 205, 206
   casualties, North Vietnamese, xv–xvii, 3, 19, 98, 184, 205, 206
   commander, North Vietnam (An), 4, 11, 21, 37, 38–39, 68, 91, 92
   commander, North Vietnam (Man), 34–37
   commander, U.S. (Moore), 4, 7–13, 19–20, 77–78, 170, 184–85
   comparison of opponents, 4
   conditions, 89–90, 115
   Congressional Medal of Honor and other awards, xvii, 79, 200
   draftees in battle, 4, 5, 78
   firepower, U.S., 9
   as Forest of the Screaming Souls, xix, 17, 111
   Galloway at, xviii, xix, 4, 9–10, 78
   Hao's poem, 126–27
   historian Phuong, after-action report, 20, 28–29
   Huey's assigned to operation, 6
   Huey transport of U.S. troops, 7, 8, 9, 10, 87, 133
   Jack Smith's account, 116–18
   Landing Zone (LZ) Albany, xv, 7, 11, 11–13, 38–39, 63, 64, 113–27, 123, 124, 206–7
   Landing Zone (LZ) Columbus, 11

Ia Drang Valley, battles of *(cont.)*
    Landing Zone (LZ) X-Ray, xv, 3,
        4, 6–7, 10, 11, 12, 19, 29, 36,
        38, 39, 50–51, 53, 77, 85–86,
        88–99, 97, 101–11, 114, 121,
        122, 124, 133–34, 170, 171,
        172–73, 205–6, 212, 224
    Landing Zone (LZ) Yankee, 88
    location, 4, 5
    "Lost Platoon," 90–92, 97
    monument planned, 149
    Moore and Galloway's return
      to (1993), xvii, 1–4, 17, 22,
      41–69
    Moore's command post, 8, 95,
      107
    Moore's orders, 5
    napalm drop, 107, 120
    night on battlefield (1993), 99,
      101–11
    non-commissioned officers,
      U.S., 5, 6
    officers, North Vietnamese, 53
    Plumley in, 6, 7, 77–78, 88, 95
    psychological effects on sur-
      vivors, xix–xx, 15, 50–51,
      94–95, 110, 115, 116–18,
      155, 201
    recovery of bodies (1966), 12,
      124
    scouting of, U.S., 6
    Sgt. Eade's account, 118–21
    song about, 67
    tactics and strategy, North
      Vietnamese, 35–37
    troop strength, 4, 5, 6, 184–85
    veteran reunions, 80–81, 116,
      199–201
    victory claimed, North Viet-
      namese, 36–37
Imploding Man, The: Back Home
    from Vietnam (Gwin), 64

improvised explosive devices (IED),
    xix
Indochina War, 34, 44, 55, 69
    ambush at Mang Yang Pass,
      67–68, 137
    ambush of Group Mobile 100,
      Chu Dreh Pass, 147–48
    American financing of, 45,
      130–31
    burial of soldiers, 68
    Dien Bien Phu (*see* Dien Bien Phu)
    failure of French command to
      understand the enemy, 137
    fort near Plei Me Camp, 6
    French forts, 61
    Giap's analysis, 189
    last engagement, 147–48
    lessons of French to American
      leadership, 22, 26, 31, 45,
      67–68, 130, 131
    Moore's study of, 45, 129–30
Iraq War, xviii–xix
    casualties, American, 195
    cost of, 194
    as failure of leadership, xx,
      191–92
    getting out of, 192
    as mistake, 193–97
    risk caused by, 194

Jakarta, Indonesia, 59
Johns, Barbara Geoghegan, 200
Johnson, Lyndon, 32, 200
Johnson, Wilbert, 119

kairos, 211
Kennedy, Col. Glen, 200
Khmer Rouge, 2, 68, 97, 104
Kinnard, Maj. Gen. Harry W. O.,
    123
Kipling, Rudyard, 27–28
Knowles, Brig. Gen. Richard, 123

Korea
 Moore in (1969) and situation
  with 7th Infantry, 173–78
 postwar occupation, 79,
  173–78
 racial tensions and drug use,
  U.S. military, 174–78
 Sukchon, 76
 Tongduchon, 174–78
Korean War, 131–32
 casualties, 190, 192
 as failure of diplomacy, 192
 French in, 67
 Moore in, 69, 74, 131–32, 133,
  165, 192, 217
 Old Baldy, 192
 Plumley in, 74, 75, 76
 Pork Chop Hill, 139, 192
 trench warfare, 131–32, 138
 U.S. weapons captured by
  Chinese, 45

Larsen, Lt. Gen. Stanley "Swede,"
 123–24
Lawrence, Lt. Jim, 67
leadership, 157–85, 189. See also
  war
 choosing a commander in chief,
  196–97
 complacency and inattention,
  danger of, 172
 constantly training and improv-
  ing, 182–83
 cover-up in Vietnam and failure
  of, 122–24
 creating the future, 165–66
 decision-making methods, 161
 first steps when put in new
  position, 173, 176–77
 four points for harnessing discipline, 165
 Gen. Robert E. Lee, 171

"influence situations in your
  favor," 163
intuition plus analysis in
  decision-making, 161
judgment, 170–71
lessons of the French in Indochina ignored, 22, 26, 31,
  45, 67–68, 130, 131
listening to staff, 74
love and, 168–69, 195–96
loyalty and, 166, 168–69, 178,
  182
maxim on "Nothing's wrong,"
  171–72
Moore's principles of, 166–67
My Lai massacre as failure of,
  56
NCOs as, 73, 74, 76, 178
never overreact, 180
"Never quit," 163
never say no to yourself, 162
North Vietnamese, 69
planning and reducing risk,
  169–70
positive, upbeat persona, 175
"push the power down,"
  181–82
reservations and doubt, 161
"skunk at the picnic," need for,
  171
"stack the deck" and questions
  to ask oneself, 163–64
on stress, 181
Sun Tzu on, 169
three demands a senior executive must meet, 164
trust, earning, 183–85
trusting one's instincts, 158–59,
  173, 209
ultimate responsibility and, 74
U.S., Vietnam War and, 67,
  107–8

leadership *(cont.)*
  Vietnam War, no explanation
    for, 108
  war chosen by men who don't
    know war, xx
  wars as failure of, xx, 188
  workable plan, need for,
    164–65
Lee, Gen. Robert E., 171
Levy, Tom, 99
Little Bighorn, 8, 67
Longstreet, Gen. James, 171
Lose, Doc Randy, 91, 92

MacMillan, Bill, 99
Man, Gen. Chu Huy, 16, 20, 24,
    25, 33
  background of, 34–35, 49
  at Dien Bien Phu, 33, 34–35,
    133, 142
  meeting with, 1991, 21–22, 33–37
  meeting with, 1993, 48–49
  meeting with, 1999, 144
Mang Yang Pass, 67–68, 137
Marm, Col. Walter J. "Joe," xvii,
    200, 208
McDade, Lt. Col. Robert "Bob,"
    11–13, 114
McNamara, Robert, 196
Metsker, Capt. Tom (S-2, intelli-
    gence officer), 8, 88
MIAs, 27, 60–61, 87
Michaellis, John H., 173–74
Montagnards, 1, 68, 152
Moore, Cecile, 218, 229
Moore, David, 218, 220–21, 229
Moore, Greg, 217, 229
Moore, Lt. Gen. Harold G. "Hal,"
    72–74
  advice to men, not to celebrate
    killing, 19–20, 49
  background of, 69, 217–18

battle at Ia Drang, 4, 7–11,
    19–20, 77–78, 87–92,
    133–34
  as commander 1st Air Cavalry,
    31, 182
  desire to talk with North Viet-
    namese commanders, 20–21
  determination and perseverance
    of, 102, 157–60, 162–63
  evolution of book, 14–17
  at Fort Ord, California, 178–81
  friendship with General An, 68,
    69, 98–99
  handling of antiwar demonstra-
    tors, 179–80
  Iraq War and, 193–97
  An Khe base memories, 64–67
  in Korea, 69, 74, 131–32, 133,
    165, 173–78, 192, 217
  on leadership, 157–85
  at Mang Yang Pass, 67–68
  marriage and children, 214–25
  meets Galloway, 9–10
  meets Giap, 31–33, 44–47, 130
  NCOs and, 71–72
  night at Ia Drang battlefield,
    99, 101–11
  in Occupied Japan, 69
  as paratrooper, 181–82
  planning for an operation, 165
  prayer at Ia Drang, 98
  recovery of bodies from Ia
    Drang (1966), 12, 124
  retirement from Army, 14–15
  return to Ia Drang (1993), xvii,
    1–4, 17, 22, 41–69, 86–123,
    147–51, 155
  return to Pleiku (1993), 83–86
  return to Vietnam (1990),
    15–16, 20–33
  return to Vietnam (1991), 22,
    33–40

return to Vietnam (1999), 22,
134–45
Schwarzkopf and, xi, xii
stress and, 181
study of French in Indochina,
45, 129–30
Vietnamese visa problems,
23–24
visit to An's widow, 142–44
visit to Dien Bien Phu (1999),
130, 134–35, 140–42
war, beliefs about, 187–201
at West Point, 68, 72–74, 132,
157–63
West Point farewell speech,
168–69, 195–96
Moore, Julia Compton "Julie,"
132, 203, 214–25
comforting families of lost
soldiers, 203–4, 215–16
courage of, 222–23
death of, 222
film of We Were Soldiers and,
221–22
Moore, Julie, 218, 229
Moore, Steve, 217, 220, 229
Muoi, Do, 16, 27
My Lai massacre, 55–56

Nadal, Capt. Tony (later Col.), 8,
14, 42, 47, 84, 90, 227
Navarre, Gen. Henri, 47, 134–36
Newcomb, Arthur W., 157
Nightline (TV program), 115,
117
NVA (North Vietnamese Army).
See also PAVN (People's
Army of Vietnam)
33rd Regiment, 114
66th Regiment, 114
massacre of civilians after fall
of Saigon, 148

troops in Chu Pong Massif, 5
U.S. helicopters and, 29

187th Airborne Regimental
Combat Team, 76
173rd Airborne, 68

Page, Tim, 23, 24
PAVN (People's Army of Vietnam)
32nd Regiment, 3
33rd Regiment, 3, 12, 114
66th Regiment, 3, 114
66th Regiment, 7th Battalion,
85
66th Regiment, 8th Battalion,
11, 12
316th Division, 34
casualties, 3
demobilization, 68
as peasant army, 37, 45
soldier's kit, 85
studying of American tactics,
28–29
troops in Chu Pong Massif, 6
Peroddy, Sgt. Maj. Don, 178,
179
Persian Gulf War, xi, xviii, 17,
192, 195
casualties, American, 190
Phillips, WO Jesse, 87
Phuong, Gen. Hoang, 20, 22
account of Landing Zone
X-Ray battle, 29, 39–40
background of, 49
meeting with, 1990, 21, 28–30
meeting with, 1991, 22, 39–40
Piroth, Col. Charles, 136–37
Plei Me Camp, 6, 10, 35, 36, 88
Plumley, Deurice, 77, 80, 88–89
Plumley, Sgt. Maj. Basil L., 41–42,
47, 71, 72, 75–81, 102, 110,
125–26, 171, 227

Plumley, Sgt. Maj. Basil L. *(cont.)*
    Ia Drang battle, 6, 7, 77–78,
        88, 95
    An Khe base, 65–66
Poley, Clinton, 200
Powell, Gen. Colin, 166, 193
PRC-25 field radio, 85–86
PTSD (posttraumatic stress disor-
        der), xvii

Quang, Nguyen Cong, 24, 228

Random House publishers, 17
Rather, Dan, 151
Reagan, Ronald, 108
Renwick, Bruce, 99
Rescorla, Lt. Cyril R. "Rick," 67,
        203
    background of, 207–9, 212–14
    as hero of 9/11, 204–5, 208–11,
        214
    iconic photo of, 206, 212
    platoon leader, 2/7 Bravo Com-
        pany, Vietnam, 205–7
Rescorla, Susan, 210–11, 213–14
Rice, Jim, 87
Roosevelt, Franklin D., 159
Roosevelt, Teddy, 148
Rowe, Nicholas, 25
Rumsfeld, Donald H., 191, 196

Saigon/Ho Chi Minh City, 56–57
    changes and growth, 149–55
    fall of, 4, 22, 35, 36, 58, 68
    girlie bars of Tu Do, 153
    thirtieth anniversary of fall of,
        153–54
    traffic, 152–53
Savage, Sgt. Ernie, 42, 47, 90,
        91–92, 97, 227
Sawyer, Forrest, 22, 42, 84, 99,
        115

Schwarzkopf, Gen. H. Norman,
        xi–xiii
    Persian Gulf War and, xii
September 11 (9/11) terrorist
        attacks, 193–94
    casualties, 194
    Morgan Stanley offices, 204,
        208–10
    Rick Rescorla as hero during,
        204–5, 208–11, 214
7th Cavalry, xv, 185
    1st Battalion, 4, 5, 10
    1st Battalion, Alpha (A) Com-
        pany, 8, 14, 38, 41–42
    1st Battalion, Bravo (B) Com-
        pany, 7, 10, 38, 42, 96
    1st Battalion, Charlie (C) Com-
        pany, 78, 96, 105–6, 172–73
    2nd Battalion, 9, 11–13, 39, 42,
        122, 206
    2nd Battalion, Alpha (A) Com-
        pany, 63, 64, 113, 118
    2nd Battalion, Bravo (B)
        Company, 9, 77–78, 90–92,
        205–7
    2nd Battalion, Charlie (C)
        Company, 86, 113, 124, 125
    history of, 8
    marching tune, 149
7th Infantry Division, 174–78
Sheehan, Neil, 32
Shucart, William, 211
Smith, Howard K., 48, 118
Smith, Jack, 42, 44, 47–48, 86,
        113, 115, 121, 155, 227
    death of, 118
    speaking on Landing Zone
        Albany battle and effects of
        experience, 116–18
South Vietnamese army, xii, 35,
        36, 62
    18th Division, 150

INDEX

Spanish-American War, 192
Special Forces A-Team Camp, Plei
    Me village, 6, 10, 35, 36, 88
Stancil, WO Ken, 87
Stowe, Madeleine, 221, 222
Street Without Joy (Fall), 129
Sullivan, Stanley, 212
Sun Tzu, 137, 169

tanks, xii, xvii
    at Dien Bien Phu (French
        M-24), 135, 140
    Iraq War, 194
    left in Vietnam, 61
    M1A1 Abrams, xviii
    Persian Gulf War, 190
    Russian, 44
Thach, Nguyen Co, 16, 27
Thai, Quyen, 42
They Were Young and Brave (TV
    documentary), 5, 22, 41–42,
    63, 95–96, 115, 155, 228
Thompson, Hunter, 151
Thuoc, Col. Vu Dinh, 53, 85–86, 87,
    122, 142, 144–45, 149, 228
Tien, Le, 31, 142
Trinh, Le Xuan, 16, 27
Tully, Lt. Col. Bob, 11
24th Infantry Division, xi, xviii
23rd Infantry
    2nd Battalion, 76
    Battle Group, 76
229th Assault Helicopter Battal-
    ion, Bravo Company, 10, 87

United Press International (UPI),
    151
    Galloway with, xi, 10
U.S. Army
    1st Cavalry Division, 3, 6, 11,
        12, 13, 15, 29, 31, 36, 62,
        63, 65, 78–79, 149

1st Cavalry Division (Airmo-
    bile), 3, 28, 123, 182
1st Corps, 79
2nd Corps, 79
2nd Infantry Division, 76, 79
3rd Infantry Division, 76
4th Infantry Division, 68
5th Cavalry, 11, 42, 113, 124, 206
7th Cavalry, xv, 4, 5, 7, 8, 9, 10,
    11–13, 14, 38, 39, 41–42, 63,
    64, 74, 77–78, 90–92, 96,
    105–6, 113, 118, 122, 124,
    125, 149, 185, 205–7
7th Infantry Division, 174–78
8th Army, 173, 177–78
11th Airborne Division, 76
23rd Infantry 2nd Battalion, 76
23rd Infantry Battle Group, 76
24th Infantry Division, xi, xviii
82nd Airborne Division, 76,
    217, 220
173rd Airborne, 68
187th Airborne Regimental
    Combat Team, 76
229th Assault Helicopter Bat-
    talion, 10, 87
change from draftee to all-vol-
    unteer, xviii, 180–81
NCOs, 71–81
officers' career trajectory,
    72–73
radio, PRC-25, 85–86
Special Forces A-Team, 6
telegram notification of sol-
    dier's death, 101, 108, 203,
    215–16
U.S. Military College at West
    Point, xii, 47, 68, 72–74,
    132, 157–63, 218
    cemetery, 195
    Moore's farewell speech,
        168–69, 195–96

USMS *Maurice Rose*, 54
U.S. News & World Report, 17, 23
   cover article on Ia Drang, 2, 5, 15–16, 21
   National Magazine Award, 16

Veterans Administration, xvi–xvii
Victoria, queen of England, 194
Viet Cong, 54
   massacre of civilians after fall of Saigon, 148
Viet Minh, 22, 34, 60, 68–69, 129, 189
   ambush of Group Mobile 100, 67
   at Dien Bien Phu, 44–47, 130, 135–37, 138 (*see also* Dien Bien Phu)
Vietnam, country of (*see also* Vietnam War)
   America's shared history with, 26
   army officers, continuing service of, 33
   attacked by Chinese, 69
   Ban Me Thuot, 148
   Bien Hoa, 150
   Bong Son Plain, 62, 207
   Cam Ranh Bay, 149–50
   capitalism, modern, in, 43, 151–52
   Catecka Tea Plantation, 9
   Central Highlands, xi, xv, 1, 3, 16, 35, 63, 68, 152, 207
   Chu Lai air base removed, 54–55
   Chu Pong Massif, 5, 6, 11, 21, 33, 36, 38, 88, 97
   contemporary, 43, 53–54, 56, 57–62, 63, 64, 65, 68, 149–52
   Danang air base today, 53–54

   diplomatic recognition and most-favored-nation trade status sought, 2, 26–27
   Duc Co, 110
   economic boom, 42–43, 149–51
   French in, 22, 31, 34, 45–47, 60, 61, 67–68, 129–30, 134, 137, 147–48 (*see also* Dien Bien Phu)
   Hanoi (*see* Hanoi)
   Hong Kong Mountain, 65
   hotels, seedy, 62, 83–84
   An Khe base, 84
   lessons of the French ignored by American leaders, 26, 31, 45, 67–68, 130, 131
   Mang Yang Pass, 67–68
   military cemeteries, 60, 97–98, 141
   modern revolutionary movement, 30
   modern technology in, 153
   Nha Trang, 149
   nuoc mam, 59
   Phan Thiet, 150
   Pleiku, 3, 6, 10, 38, 68, 79, 83–86, 110, 122, 125
   Plei Me village, 6, 10, 97
   port city of Qui Nhon, 54
   Quang Ngai province, 55
   Qui Nhon, 62
   Saigon/Ho Chi Minh City (*see* Saigon/Ho Chi Minh City)
   smells of, 59
   thousand years of war, xiii, 25
   tigers of, 96, 104, 105, 148
   trade with China and the U.S., 151–52
   "two-step" viper, 104
   village life, 57
   Xuan Loc, 150

INDEX

Vietnamese Communist Party, 43

Vietnam Historical Museum, 25

Vietnam Memorial, Washington, D.C., 106

Vietnam Military Museum, 42, 44

Vietnam War, xiii, 192–93
  American POWs, 140
  as "American War," 56
  Ap Bac battle, Mekong Delta, 31–32
  B-2 Front (North Vietnamese), 35
  B-52 bombing raids, Christmas, 1972, 40
  battle for Ban Me Thuot, 36
  Battle of Hill 875 (Dak To), 68
  Battle of Xuan Loc, 150
  bloodiest battle, xvi (See Ia Drang Valley, battles of)
  C-123 crash, 63
  casualties, American, 107, 190, 193
  casualties, Vietnamese and Cambodian, 107, 190
  Chu Lai air base, 54–55
  Danang, 28, 36, 35, 53–54
  draftees sent to, 56, 78, 180
  Duc Co, xi, 88
  erasure of all evidence of, 60–62
  failure of leadership and, 55–56, 193
  fall of Saigon and South Vietnam, 4, 22, 35, 36, 58, 68, 153–54
  fuel-air bomb used, 150
  futility of, 62
  Giap's analysis, 189
  H and I fire, 65–66
  history's view of, 108
  Ho Chi Minh Trail, xv, 4, 22, 28, 37, 85, 136
  Hue massacre, 55
  An Khe base, 64–67, 87
  An Khe Pass, 63
  lack of officer training, 56
  learning from, xx, 45, 196
  MIA issue, 27
  Moore and Galloway's quest for truth, 2
  Moore's plan for an operation, 165
  My Lai massacre, 55–56
  North Vietnamese killing of U.S. prisoners, 86
  North Vietnamese killing of U.S. wounded, 44, 50
  North Vietnam generals, 16 (see also specific generals)
  North Vietnam tactics and strategy, 35–37
  Operation Masher–White Wing, 62, 63
  Operation Starlight, 35
  as "people's war," 32
  Pleiku Campaign (Tay Nguyen Campaign), xv–xvi, xvii, 13, 22, 34, 35 (see also Ia Drang Valley battles)
  Plei Me Camp, 6, 10, 35, 36, 88
  POW camp, Mekong Delta, 24–25
  press coverage, 55–56
  Qui Nhon, 85th Evacuation Hospital at, 123
  Qui Nhon, troop landing at, 54, 62, 87
  refugees after fall of Saigon, 148
  reporters and newsmen in, 10, 55, 151 (see also Galloway, Joseph L.)
  resolution of Vietnamese opposition, 31, 145

Vietnam War *(cont.)*
  soldiers, both sides, as blood
    brothers, 40
  start of U.S., 7
  Tet Offensive, 32, 55
  "Trail of Tears," 148
  tunnels and trenches, 138–39
  U.S. technology vs. peasant
    army, 37
  U.S. veterans, unresolved anger,
    44
  veterans from both sides meet-
    ing, 48–51

Wallenius, Jon, 200
war, 187–201
  American reluctance to start,
    historically, 192
  on American soil, 190
  doctrine of preemptive military
    action, 191–92
  Erasmus on, 195
  as failure of leadership, xx,
    55–56, 188, 192, 193
  as last resort, 188
  no "noble" war, 108
  psychological effects on survi-
    vors, 155
  soldier's motivation in, 108
  Sun Tzu on, 137
  tests to meet, questions to
    answer before committing
    to, 188–89
  trench warfare, 131, 132,
    137–39
  World War II as necessary war,
    189–90
War, The (TV documentary), 155
War of 1812, 190
weapons, North Vietnamese
  105mm howitzers, 45, 136
  AK-47s, 8

antiaircraft guns, 136
  Katyusha rockets, 136
weapons, U.S.
  40mm M79 grenades, 91, 116
  105mm howitzers, 9, 65–66
  flechettes, 60
  fuel-air bomb, 150
  M16 machine guns, 7
  M60 machine guns, 7
  rocket-firing helicopter gun-
    ships, 9
Westmoreland, Gen. William C.,
    122–24
We Were Soldiers (film), xvi
  Julia Moore's influence on,
    221–22
*We Were Soldiers Once . . . and
    Young* (Moore and Gallo-
    way), xii, xvi, 4, 41, 76–77,
    200, 206, 218–19
  evolution of book, 14–17
  translated into Vietnamese, 2,
    49
  World War I, 190
  World War II
  Americans in, 190
  attack on Pearl Harbor, 159,
    172
  Battle of the Bulge, 172
  Bishop in, 178
  Burns's documentary on, 155
  casualties, 190
  casualties, American, 190
  combat jumps of 82nd Airborne
    (Sicily, Salerno, Normandy,
    Market Garden), 76
  failure of leadership and, 172
  German invasion of Poland,
    190
  as necessary war, 189–90
  Plumley in, 74, 75, 76
Wrong, Terry, 41, 42, 99, 228

PHOTOGRAPHY CREDITS

1. U.S. Army photograph
2. Courtesy Hal Moore
3. Courtesy Hal Moore
4. Courtesy Hal Moore
5. Courtesy Hal Moore
6. Courtesy Hal Moore
7. Courtesy Joe Galloway
8. Courtesy Joe Galloway
9. Courtesy Joe Galloway
10. Photograph by Joe Galloway
11. Photograph by Joe Galloway
12. Photograph by Joe Galloway
13. Photograph by Joe Galloway
14. Photograph by Joe Galloway
15. Courtesy Joe Galloway
16. Photograph by Joe Galloway
17. Photograph by Joe Galloway
18. Photograph courtesy Bill Beck
19. Photograph by Joe Galloway
20. Photograph by Joe Galloway
21. Courtesy Hal Moore
22. Courtesy Hal Moore
23. Photograph by Joe Galloway
24. Photograph by Bill Beck
25. Courtesy Hal Moore
26. Courtesy Hal Moore
27. Courtesy Hal Moore
28. Courtesy Susan Rescorla
29. Courtesy Susan Rescorla
30. Courtesy Susan Rescorla
31. Courtesy Hal Moore
32. Courtesy Hal Moore
33. Photograph by Joe Galloway
34. Courtesy Hal Moore
35. Courtesy Joe Galloway